THE TILE BOOK

DECORATING WITH FIRED EARTH

THE TILE BOOK

ELIZABETH HILLIARD

SOMA

This edition first published in Great Britain in 1999 by
Pavilion Books Limited.
North American edition published in 1999
by Soma Books, by arrangement
with Pavilion Books.
Soma Books is an imprint of Bay
Books & Tapes, 555 De Haro Street
No. 220, San Francisco, CA 94107.

Interior designed by David Fordham
Picture research by Mary-Jane Gibson
North American editor: Jain Lemos

Library of Congress cataloging-in-publication data on file with publisher.

ISBN I-57959-020-9

Color reproduction by DP Graphics
Printed and bound in Singapore by Tien Wah Press

1 3 5 7 9 10 8 6 4 2

Distributed by Publishers Group West

CONTENTS

INTRODUCTION

O F ALL THE MATERIALS that we so lovingly use to decorate our homes and make them practical, safe places that also look beautiful, none has proved so everlasting as the tile. Fashions in interior decoration come and go—wallpaper versus paint, fitted carpeting versus bare floors, chandeliers versus hidden spotlights—but the tile is always present.

The reason is not hard to divine. Across the world and over many centuries, the tile has established itself as a practical, hardwearing tool in the decoration of buildings inside and out. From the earthy, organic quality of English medieval slipware to the brilliant colors of maiolica tiles made in seventeenth-century Mexico; from the mellow comfort of antique French terra-cotta to the twentieth century's individual pieces made by craftspeople across the world—tiles have proved themselves timeless. Many of these historical types of tile, such as Mexican maiolica, are still made today and exported to the continents of the world. Tile art has provided a link between nations and down the generations.

Artists and crafts people have also enjoyed using the tile, and the luscious colors and finishes that can be achieved with firing, as a vehicle for artistic expression. The walls of kitchens and bathrooms in particular, of all the rooms in the home, are showplaces for such tiles. But floor tiles can make an equally valuable contribution, especially in hot climates (where they are cool), cold climates (where they are laid on a solid base incorporating underfloor heating), family homes (where the right type is wonderfully practical and long lasting—even improving with age) and small spaces (where clever use of tiles on a floor can unify a series of small rooms, or be laid to create an illusion of greater width).

Just as tile art is perennial, so on a more modest scale has this book proved to be. The first edition was published around the world and has become something of a classic, to the extent that this new edition is called for. Freshly designed and with new photographs that bring it up to date, *The Tile Book* is superbly equipped to carry the story of tiles and the message of their beauty and practicality into the twenty-first century.

OPPOSITE The Arab Hall at Leighton House, built in London in 1886 for the artist Frederick Lord Leighton, decorated with antique Islamic tiles and a mosaic frieze by Walter Crane.

SECTION I:

HISTORY AND DESIGN

THE ISLAMIC WORLD

THE STORY OF TILES in the ancient and Islamic worlds does not follow a neat straight line in time and place. Instead, it is as colorful and intricate as the design on an elaborate Islamic tile, leaping about from country to country and from century to century. The ancient Egyptians faced buildings with bricks coated with colored glaze, and the Abyssinians decorated monuments with relief animals formed from glazed tiles. In some periods the tiles popularity wanes, and with it the whole state of the industry, while in others the inventiveness of designers and artisans and the imagination of patrons and architects lift the slab of baked earth to heights of brilliance. At all times, however, the tile depends on a peaceful and stable political atmosphere of the type in which all arts and crafts have the best chance of thriving; in which the attention of rulers is focused not on fighting wars but on glorifying themselves and their gods by embellishing palaces and places of worship.

The most brilliant moment in the tile making industry came in Turkey in the middle of the sixteenth century, under the rule of the sultans of the Ottoman Empire and, in particular, Sultan Suleiman the Magnificent. Many of the buildings created during this period can still be seen today, monuments both to patrons and to craftsmen. The sultans were enthusiastic patrons, and their program of building magnificent mosques and palaces

ABOVE This panel of cross-shaped and star-shaped tiles found in Kashan in central Iran is believed to date from the second half of the fourteenth century.

RIGHT This arrangement appears frequently on tiled Islamic buildings. The hexagons enclose lively flower forms and are separated by triangles of dark blue.

coincided with a steady improvement in the tile makers' technical and artistic achievements. Tile making was part of a much wider ceramics industry and sometimes tiles were eclipsed by utility ceramics—dishes, bowls, jugs and other vessels for practical use—but the sixteenth century was not one of those periods.

Like other artisans, tile makers were an itinerant breed, moving between cities and countries according to the work offered by each place. The two centers of the tile making industry were outside Istanbul itself, in Iznik and Kutahya. Designs were provided by artists at court and then sent out to Iznik and Kutahya, where samples were made. In the case of at least one commission it is known that the two towns were actually in competition with each other; Iznik won.

As far as we know, the tiles from Iznik and Kutahya were made from local clay of excellent quality which was quarried at or near the factories, and fired in kilns powered by the burning of timber, of which there was plenty in the immediate countryside. Today, kilns and other elements of mechanization may be powered by electricity or modern generators, yet access to the raw material, clay, is still an important consideration in the siting of tile factories. All over the world, tile making factories dig the clay from surface pits in their own back yards, transporting it only a few hundred yards and processing it directly, or after minimal blending, without complicated purification techniques. Clay could be called nature's own manufacturing material.

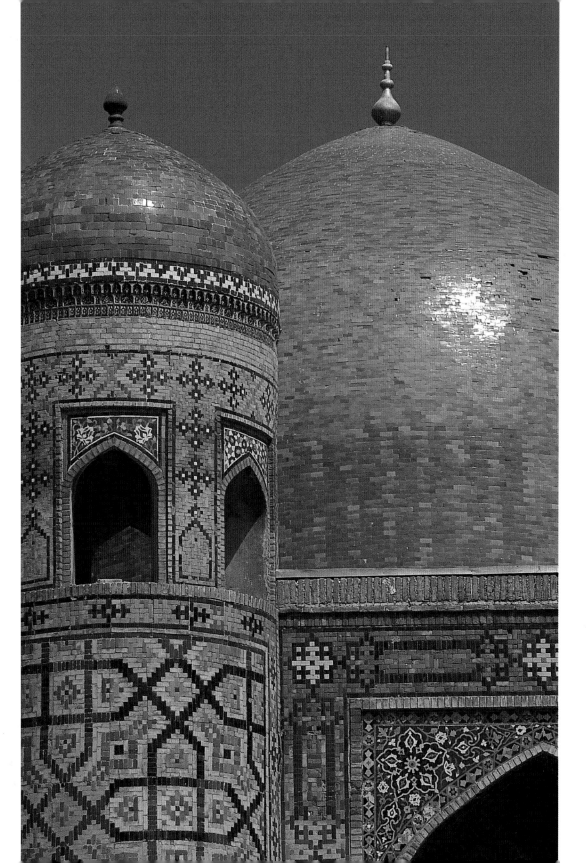

RIGHT The breathtaking sight of tiled domes gleaming in the sun. The walls of this mosque at Samarkano in Uzbekistan in Central Asia have a variety of tiled decoration linked to each other by the predominance of shades of blue.

LEFT These exquisite tiles and tiled panels in a palace in Istanbul bear witness to the great artistic and technical skills of Iznik craftsmen. Today's Iznik tiles (of which the border design opposite is an example) are the descendants of that tradition.

The clay of Iznik was white when fired and offered an ideal background for a brilliant white underglaze, against which colored decoration stood out well. In the fourteenth century, increased trade with China brought Chinese ceramics into the country and made blue and white decoration fashionable, a combination that suited Iznik products.

The white glaze achieved by the Iznik tilers was of marvelous quality, and did not crackle when fired. Black or green and blue decoration on white was popular, as was black under a limpid turquoise glaze. Shapes of tiles included the predictable square and other, more elaborate shapes, inherited from previous periods of tile making, which we think of today as being typically Islamic: the hexagon, sometimes with plain-colored triangles between, and the eight-pointed star showing flowers and birds, which was used in combination with a geometrically-decorated pointed cross. Stencils were used to enable the craftsmen to reproduce designs accurately.

From the town of Iznik, finished work was transported to Istanbul by first being taken overland on horseback to the port of Karamorsel, and then by boat to the capital. The total time needed between manufacturing the tiles and seeing them installed on a building was only a matter of weeks.

Tiles were used on the outside and inside of buildings, covering whole walls, façades and domes, not merely in decorative panels placed here and there. The overall effect is stunning. Outdoors, in brilliant sunshine, tiled buildings radiate color, the white and blue glazes reflecting light in a way which would outshine even a building covered in real turquoise. Decoration on the tiles was conceived overall as well as in detail, so that there is as much to look at and reflect upon at a distance as there is on close inspection. Up close, you can read the inscriptions, enshrined in particular panels, or leading the eye around the building, and see in detail the lively portrayal of trees and flowers. From a distance, the eye

RIGHT One of the most visually appealing aspects of an impressive tiled interior, such as this one in a mosque in Istanbul, is the way that it has been designed both as a whole and in every fine detail.

follows the decoration upwards through intricate arabesques to the higher reaches where individual images blend into the soaring curves of the architecture.

Besides two blues—a vivid turquoise and a deeper shade similar to indigo—colors on Iznik tiles include green and black. But the color that above all others characterizes Iznik tiles at their pinnacle of artistic achievement is red. Variously described since then as "radiant tomato-red" or "sealing-wax red," the color was a technical breakthrough that demonstrated the skill of the tile makers and gave the designers much greater scope. Until now, the only achievable red was more like a shade of brown, after firing, due to chemical reactions in the glaze. The tile makers of Iznik solved the problem by producing first a slightly mottled version, then a pure brilliant red, which they applied thickly for maximum effect. Not only was the color splendid in its own right, but it made a vivid contrast to existing blues and greens, and in particular to

RIGHT These panels use tiles with an identical or mirror-image design to create a larger pattern.

OPPOSITE A North African interior. Pool, walls and pillars are faced with tiles with contemporary interpretations of Islamic designs. The floor is covered with marble tiles.

another new color, a viridian green. Manganese, a brownish-purple color, was in most cases dropped from the palette, because it was dull by comparison with the new red and because it did not contrast well with it.

Designers made the most of the opportunities offered by the range of colors now available. Reflecting the Turkish tastes of the period, tiles were decorated with swirling patterns, often incorporating realistic portrayals of peonies, pomegranate flowers, roses, hyacinths, violets, cypress trees, vines, birds and even imitations of marble. Many of these motifs also appeared in contemporary carpets and textiles and other products of the decorative and applied arts. This homogeneity was not surprising, since the same court artists were supplying designs for these and for the tiles of Iznik and Kutahya.

It was not only the grand palaces and mosques, designed as a reflection of earthly and spiritual power and glory, that were decorated with tiles. Domestic quarters such as the harem were clad in tiles, as were fountains, libraries, courtyards and the more wealthy homes. The Sultan is even reputed to have decorated one of his barges with tiles. Tiles were expensive and their use was a reflection of status, but they were available to any wealthy person who could pay for them. They were not simply confined to walls, although this is where they were most used. Window openings, for instance, were given ceramic surrounds and even filled with open-work lattice tiles.

The burgeoning success of the Islamic tile industry could not be maintained indefinitely. One of the signals that all was not well occurred in the middle of the seventeenth century, with a change in tone of the red and other color glazes. The red lost its vigor and became dull and brownish, while other colors also became muted and muddied. The quality of glazes deteriorated and designs also lost their edge, becoming sketchier and more monotonous and repetitive. One of the causes of this deterioration was the weakening of court patronage. The Turkish Empire was no longer rock solid and the sultans' attention turned from their surroundings in Istanbul to the wider world where their power was under threat.

By 1648 only nine tile making factories remained, whereas in around 1600 there had been approximately three hundred. Iznik tile makers did not sit by idly and watch their industry decline; they sought other markets, and gained commissions from farther afield, from countries such as Greece. But the lack of sufficiently big local and foreign orders and the deterioration in the quality of the tiles were problems too great to overcome. By the end of the seventeenth century the formerly great tile industry in Iznik had almost faded away. It did not vanish completely, however. Enough craftsmen remained for an attempt to be made to revive the industry, not in Iznik but in Istanbul, in the early eighteenth century. The attempt was not a great success. It proved impossible to recapture the combination of vivid colors on a pure ground with a flawlessly clear overglaze, and the introduction of new colors, such as a lurid yellow, seemed to detract from rather than add to the intended effect.

LEFT A garden is the nearest place to heaven in Muslim thinking; this one in Marrakesh in Morocco has a cool tiled alcove with a bench where one may sit and contemplate its beauty.

An even more significant difference in these eighteenth-century tiles was the approach to design. One of the elements that made earlier tile-covered buildings so magnificent was the way in which the decoration was conceived as a whole, over the entire building. Eighteenth-century designers tended to focus on individual tiles, which resulted in cruder, repetitive patterns rather than the great dramatic swirls and schemes that romped across the monuments of previous ages.

The Turkish people did not lose their love of decorating with tiles during this period, and are known to have imported quantities of blue and white tiles from Holland in the middle of the eighteenth century. Another development gave a bizarre twist to the history of the Islamic tile: it was hijacked, by Christians, and in particular by the wealthy Armenian Christians who had fled to Turkey to escape the upheavals of war in their own country. When they returned to Armenia, they gave generously to their churches, and splendid church interiors came into being, created with tiles from Kutahya.

In the twentieth century, tile making in Kutahya once again experienced a resurgence, based on traditional Iznik and Islamic designs and on commissions from the authorities involved with repairing and rejuvenating Jerusalem after the First World War. Public and religious buildings, and on a smaller scale private homes, have continued to be covered with large areas of tiling, which is not considered particularly expensive and cannot be surpassed for decorative effect and practicality. From time to time, special, prestigious commissions, like the tiles made for the Hilton hotel in

Right Two details showing quite different decorative styles: robust diagonals and strong, deep colors on a wall in Tangiers, Morocco (left) and a pattern of small geometric shapes on a white ground, on an architectural detail of the Alhambra, in Granada, Spain.

Istanbul in the mid-1950s and the recently built Makkah Gate Bridge, give the industry a welcome boost.

In the history of tiles, no period is totally self-contained. Ideas and designs leapfrog across the centuries and from one culture to another, echoing the tile maker's roving quest to find work through the ages. Lusterware, for example, on which glazes have a metallic ingredient and finish, was one of the most exciting products of the Islamic ceramics industry. Luster, together with the vibrant colors and swirling vigor of the designs on fine Islamic tiles, inspired an Englishman, William De Morgan, to design and make some of the most beautiful and distinctive tiles and other ceramics of the later nineteenth century. And in 1921, an Armenian factory in Kutahya made decorated "Islamic" tiles for an inlaid sideboard by the Arts and Crafts designer C. R. Ashbee, demonstrating a continuing awareness of and interest in Eastern tiles on the part of Western designers and craftsmen.

Today, Islamic tiles are made in Turkey in a small but flourishing industry, still craft-based with a minimal amount of mechanization in the production process, and apparently depending on the enthusiasm and commitment of individual industrialists. Over the centuries, meanwhile, Islamic religion and culture spread into Europe, Africa, the East and Asia. It even progressed as far northwest as Spain, where it was taken up by the Moors. In Granada, southern Spain, the Alhambra is a dazzling monument to the effect to which tiles can be put when applied *en masse* to a building, especially when combined with water. Today in Granada, a few factories still produce tiles in the colors and designs of the fourteenth century. As always, wherever they are made the quality of modern Islamic tiles depends as much on design as on technical standards, and studies by modern designers of the best achievements of historical tiles have led to new tiles in satisfyingly clean, vigorous patterns which do no discredit to the great tradition.

MEDIEVAL TILES

IN SHIFTING OUR ATTENTION from the Islamic world to Medieval England, our focus also moves from walls down to floors. Many Arabic and other Islamic peoples were nomadic, packing up their treasured possessions and taking them with them as they traveled from place to place. One of the great traditions of the Islamic world lay in making fine carpets and rugs, which were used to cover floors and could, if necessary, be rolled up with ease and removed to the next town or camp.

By contrast, England had been an important outpost of the Roman Empire, whose technique for embellishing the floors in their palaces and grand villas was the mosaic. There are strong parallels between tiled floors and mosaic floors, although the materials involved are different. Roman mosaics were constructed from tiny squares of stone in their natural color and occasionally from colored glass, rather than from the man-made fired components that make up a tiled floor. But the reasons for laying mosaics were similar to those behind tiled floors: they were decorative and prestigious, hard-wearing and practical—all qualities which are equally valid today.

With mosaics, the small size of the pieces, and the elaborate and figurative subjects they showed, meant that the best effect was achieved by laying the pieces to follow the lines of the subject, be it a mythological god

ABOVE Tiles from St. Augustine's Abbey in Canterbury, probably made in the potteries of Tyler Hill, north of the city. Archeological discoveries suggest that potteries flourised at the beginning of the fourteenth century.

LEFT Mosaic is the technique of using many tiny square "tiles" cut from marble to create detailed patterns and pictures, as here where the face and hair of the figure show simple but realistic shading and contrasts.

or an abstract decorative motif. By contrast, medieval tiled floors used larger pieces in whole geometric shapes or squares, and the layout was correspondingly more regular.

The Romans also occasionally made floors from stone cut into shapes, rather like pieces of tile mosaic. This was called *opus sectile*. One of the few examples of this type of floor to survive in Britain can be found at the Roman palace in Fishbourne. The Romans did make tiles, but they were unglazed, utilitarian building components for roofs, wall friezes and floors. These were undecorated, and did not have the prestige either of Roman mosaic or of decorative tile pavements in medieval England.

A few Roman floor mosaics had been uncovered and were known to people in medieval England, but the source of the enthusiasm for tiled floors was more obviously contemporary. Small quantities of Spanish tiles had come into the country with travelers and tradesmen, and returning crusaders brought

with them a knowledge of and interest in Eastern tiles. English craftsmen were already sufficiently skilled in making and using lead glazes, and were able to apply this expertise to the making of floor tiles.

The deciding factor in the flowering of medieval tile art in England was probably the church. Gradually, over the centuries, it had reached an unrivaled position of power and influence, based to a great extent on the wealth that came with landowning on a large scale. Abbots and bishops became patrons of the arts, commissioning buildings which reflected the extent of their secular power as well as glorifying God. Architects and craftsmen looked as much to these churchmen for work as they did to kings and princes. Accordingly, it was in cathedrals and abbeys that many of the most magnificent tiled floors were to be found.

In the Cistercian religious settlements of England, the lay brothers and the monks themselves were a source of unpaid

RIGHT Mosaic tiles are made by arranging pieces of stone face-down in the required pattern in a frame, then fixing these in place with a mortar. Today the mortar is a cement-based compound.

BELOW Tile makers at Bawsey in Norfolk were active in the fourteenth century and contributed tiles to buildings across Norfolk, including Castle Acre Priory. This example shows a simple heraldic design.

labor in the tile industry. Among other duties, these men would lay the floors and even help make the tiles in the tilery, which specialist tile makers would construct on-site for the purpose of fulfilling a large commission. In the first decades of the thirteenth century, when the enthusiasm for tiled floors was first apparent in England, this is largely how the tiles were manufactured. It was a system that took a good part of the year to complete. Clay was dug out of the ground in the autumn months, turned in winter, and worked into tiles in spring. In the meantime, the tile making workshops and kilns were being prepared. Tile blanks were cut, then dried outdoors or in a shed kept warm with a fire, before being decorated, trimmed, glazed and fired.

In 1347, large numbers of people died from the plague known as the Black Death. This resulted in a diminution in the numbers of men in the workforce and a general impoverishment of the community, patrons and workmen alike. As a consequence, the way in which tiles were manufactured underwent a change. Commercial tileries had already existed for nearly a century, satisfying the increasing demand for tiles from people such as successful merchants, who wanted tiled floors in their most important rooms. Following the Black Death, on-site tileries virtually ceased to exist, while commercial tileries became the normal source of supply, charging customers for the transport of their tiles as well as for the tiles themselves.

The most immediately striking difference between medieval English tiles and the greatest achievements of the Islamic tile making industry is their color. In place of cool

RIGHT The most important area of the old refectory at Cleeve Abbey in Somerset was where the high table stood. The tiled pavement under the high table are decorated with three heraldic designs: the royal arms, those of the Clare family and those of the Poitou family. The floor was made to celebrate the marriage of Edmund of Cornwall.

brilliant whites, blues and greens, English medieval tiles offer warm, earthy tones of reddish-brown, clotted cream, various shades of green and a sooty black. The different colors evoke a dramatic change in atmosphere: Islamic tiles speak of hot sunlight glancing off dazzling blue domes and making patterns in the sparkling water of pools and fountains; English medieval tiles conjure up images of the mysterious dusky gloom of soaring Gothic churches, and the crackle and glow of fires indoors to keep at bay the weather and wintry landscape outside. The same contrast is true in today's homes: Islamic patterned tiles hint at sunshine and eastern sophistication; stoneware tiles in earthy colors suggest warmth and cozy slippers.

The colors of medieval tiles were the result of the lead glazes that were used in their decoration. The basic glaze turned white clay yellow, due to iron impurities in its make-up. Other metals could be added to create other colors: extra iron for a dark brown, small amounts of copper or brass for green and larger amounts for black. The final color of a decorated tile also depended on the color of the clay from which the tile was made and with which its pattern, if any, was formed. The basic glaze, for example, looked yellow on white clay, but olive-green on grey, and brown on red.

There are two elements in the decorative impact of medieval tiled floors: the shape and arrangement of the tiles, and their surface decoration. The simplest floors had square, undecorated tiles, and the next simplest had square tiles, each decorated with one of two colored glazes, which were arranged alternately in a checkerboard pattern. These became popular in the middle of the sixteenth century, right at the end of the greatest period of medieval tile art. Floors decorated in this way were part of the new interest in Italianate architecture during the sixteenth century, and contributed to the disappearance of the decorated tile.

LEFT Another heraldic
tile from Cleeve Abbey.
This one shows the royal
arms with the three
lions in the central
shield.

29

RIGHT Four tiles make up this royal coat of arms found on the floor of the Chapter House at Westminster Abbey.

OPPOSITE The Great Pavement in London's Westminster Abbey is a work of opus sectile, made using pieces of stone cut to fit a complex pattern. The designer was a member of a leading family of marble workers in Rome.

The most dramatic floors to make an impact through the shape and arrangement of the tiles were the so-called "tile mosaics." These were formed from tiles which were undecorated except for a colored lead glaze. The pieces of the tile mosaic were cut into their eventual geometric shapes before being fired, and later fitted together like a jigsaw to form an uninterrupted floor. The craftsman, monk or lay brother who laid the floor would start in the middle, so that any irregularity in the size or shape of the building could be accommodated in the borders around the edges.

One such floor which survives today was from Byland Abbey in Yorkshire and is on display in the British Museum. From a sun-like flower in the center, rings of geometric pattern radiate out until they nearly reach the edges of the floor. The patterns within the rings are bursting with vitality, though some consist of little more than simple diamonds or diagonal squares. The main band of pattern is a necklace of wheels, each with curved lozenge-shaped spokes. Each corner of the square floor, outside these concentric circles, is further decorated with an individual ringed star and two moons.

Fragments of other mid-thirteenth-century floors, one of which comes from another Yorkshire abbey called Rievaulx, further demonstrate the ingenuity of the designers of tile mosaics. One is a pattern formed entirely from dark triangles and pale diamonds; another has circles within circles connected by S-shaped curved strips; yet another has an elaborate layout of larger circles punctuated with smaller ones and containing eight-petaled flower shapes. In all the examples, the designer has made maximum impact with a limited range of colors created by lead glaze over the natural clay. Even more striking is the liveliness of the designs, which communicate a real joy in inventive use of interlocking shapes and bold patterns, and speak to us across the hundreds of years since they were created. In this sense they are totally modern.

RIGHT A detail of the floor of the Basilica of San Marco in Venice. This marble floor uses smaller squares and triangles to create added interest in alternate squares.

In thirteenth-century England there was one outstanding example of real *opus sectile* or "cut work" (the method of decorating floors by covering them with intricate patterns of cut-out shapes in stone that had been popular with the Greeks and Romans). It can still be seen today in Westminster Abbey, where King Henry III and his Abbot of Westminster, Richard de Ware, initiated the magnificent scheme of decoration completed in 1268. The King's ambassador had seen such work in Italy and been deeply impressed—so much so that de Ware was able to bring over from Rome a designer called Odoricus, a talented member of one of the highly skilled families who specialized in stone inlaid floors and who were called the Cosmati. They gave their name to the medieval version of *opus sectile*, which came to be known as "cosmati work." Much of the marble used to decorate Westminster Abbey was imported from Italy specially for the purpose. The magnificence and intricacy of this floor inspired other abbeys to attempt their own, tiled, versions.

Making and assembling tile mosaics was an exceptionally tricky and time-consuming method of covering floors, however, and by the middle of the fourteenth century the fashion had passed and no more were made. Two types of floor decoration which remained popular were two-color tiles, and relief and counter-relief tiles. The latter were mostly made by stamping the pattern into the tiles, either so that the decoration stood out (relief), or so that it was set back from the surface (counter-relief). In both cases, the person carving the wooden block used to stamp the tiles had to remember to reverse the pattern, writing or heraldic motif on his carving, so that it would come out the right way on the tile. Many tiles of the period show that this important detail could easily slip the memory of the craftsman concerned. Later, the method of stamping pattern onto tiles was used to make line patterns and pictures, and some tiles were simply incised individually by hand to achieve the same effect.

The patterned tiles that achieved greatest popularity were those with two-color decoration. They too were stamped with a pattern, which was then filled with clay of a contrastingly pale color and trimmed. Later, instead of clay in a solid state, the indentations were filled with "slip," or watered-down clay that was thickly runny. This was allowed to dry before firing. It was floors decorated with tiles like these that the Victorians uncovered and copied with such enthusiasm in the nineteenth century.

Inlaid two-color decorated tiles from this period showed a wide range of pictures of people, animals, birds, fish, heraldic symbols, mythical beasts, legendary characters, castles, plants and leaves, portrayed in a simple but lively and spirited manner. Others had abstract decoration in the form of energetically curling swirls and arabesques, and others still showed names, or various references to important church and civic officials. Decorated tiles were often laid in square or rectangular panels across a floor, divided by bands of plain tiles of a contrasting color. This way, the patterned tiles, which were more expensive, went further, and their impact was also increased by being framed.

Right A detail of the Victorian tiling of Brodsworth Hall, the magnificent stately home near Doncaster in Yorkshire.

Below Small tiles from the famous refectory floor at Cleeve Abbey in Somerset, plain strips with small decorative inserts framing square tiles decorated with slipware lions.

Other floors were designed with an overall pattern, perhaps radiating out in circles like the famous floor for the chapel of Clarendon Palace, built for Henry III, or the particularly beautiful and delicately patterned floor from Muchelney Abbey in Somerset, which the Victorians saved and resited in the parish church there. A great many beautiful inlaid tiled floors of the medieval period can still be seen today, very often surrounded by the ruins of the abbey buildings they adorned. If a reminder were needed, they would bear witness to the longevity both of this type of decoration, set into the tiles, and of tiles themselves.

MAIOLICA

OPPOSITE Miscellaneous
decorated tiles from
the sixteenth and
seventeenth centuries
have been skillfully used
in this contemporary
home in Milan, Italy,
creating an intriguing
patchwork of patterns.

IT IS EASY TO SEE AT A GLANCE the difference between medieval tiles and maiolica: a medieval tile has a rich earthy color and organic quality; a maiolica tile sparkles with brightly colored painted decoration in blue and yellow and green on a white background, and looks sophisticated and delicate. The two tiles seem worlds apart, but in fact the only thing that divides them, in the first instance, is a handful of ashes. It is the addition of oxide (ashes) of tin to the lead glaze that performs the miraculous transformation of a clay-colored tile into an opaquely white tile. The white glaze has a double effect: it conceals completely the color of the clay beneath and it provides a clean white ground, like a sheet of paper, on which the craftsman can paint to show off his bright colors to sparkling effect.

The umbrella name for tiles and ceramics decorated in this fashion is "tin-glazed ware." Maiolica (or majolica as it is sometimes called) is the name given to the wares made in the southern Mediterranean countries— Italy, Spain and Portugal—while in France it is known as *faience* and in Germany, *fayence*. The famous tin-glazed ware made much later in the Netherlands and later still in England is called delftware. The latter has special characteristics of its own, as the next chapter will show, but technically the decorative method is the same.

ABOVE Modern maiolica
tiles with an elegant
pattern based on a
traditional Italian design.

The basic square tile is made from clay and given a first, "biscuit," firing. The resulting tile is dry and porous and readily soaks up the liquid tin glaze, into which it is dipped or which is poured over it, leaving a good layer on the surface. (The tile can be dipped in water first so that less glaze is absorbed and more lies on the surface.) The decorator can then paint his patterns and pictures on to the tile, using a variety of colored glazes formed by the selective addition of yet other metals.

These metallic pigments look unexciting at this stage—dull, matte shades of grey and brown. Known as "high-temperature colors," they are subjected to a hot glaze firing, which only they can withstand, and become vibrant shades of blue (from the addition of cobalt to the glaze), yellow (antimony), red (iron), green (copper) and purple (manganese). In the eighteenth century, the range of colored decoration on tin-glazed ceramics was increased by adding, after the high temperature firing, a second layer of painted pattern using enamel colors which need firing at a lower temperature. Luster and gold decoration could also be added in a similar, second, lower temperature firing.

The origins of tin glaze go back to ancient history. From the Near East and, later, Mesopotamia, it spread to Spain and the rest of Europe via North Africa and the Islamic Empire. It also spread to Mexico, exported there by Spanish potters when it became a Spanish colony in the sixteenth century. Islamic Moors and Christians coexisted in Spain more or less peacefully for centuries until the Moors' expulsion in 1610, by which time the two cultures had become intermixed. One

ABOVE Mexico has a rich history of tile making. Here, a floor made in about 1730 to decorate San Francisco Acatepic, Puebla has terra-cotta rectangles interspersed with plain colored tiles and some with simple flower motifs.

RIGHT Tiles continue to be made today in Puebla, Mexico.

37

RIGHT A bright and colorful panel decorating the Alcazar gardens in Seville shows a goat being milked and dates from the sixteenth century.

OPPOSITE This splendid tile panel showing soldiers marching to the battle of Lepanto decorates the palace of the Marquis de Santa Cruz at Castilla-La Mancha in Portugal.

of the beneficiaries of this was the Spanish ceramic industry, which gained not only the knowledge of Islamic design, tin-glazing and luster but also substantial commissions for tiles upon which to use these skills.

From at least the early years of the eleventh century, tin-glazed wares were made in southern Spain. By the thirteenth century, when the startling new blues made possible by the addition of cobalt to glaze were introduced, Malaga was established as an important center for production. Ceramics were exported from here to countries across Europe. In the later part of the fourteenth century, the Malaga industry was given the commission that above all others has probably made Spanish tile work famous—the Alhambra in Granada.

Set high on a hill, the Alhambra is a palace of light with a magical atmosphere, even today when it is inhabited largely by crowds of tourists. Some of the tile work has been cleverly restored, but much is original. Room after room has tiled walls, dados, and archways framing magnificent views out over the hills of Andalucia or vistas within the buildings. Courtyards with pools and fountains sparkle with light reflected off tiled surrounds, pavements and pillars. In the brilliant sunshine and heat, the effect is not cold and hard but embracingly cool and serene. Visitors linger and seem eventually to drag themselves away only with great effort. The interior of the Alhambra is a unique example of how beautiful and even restful a tiled interior can be.

By the fifteenth century, Valencia had overtaken Malaga as the most successful center of the ceramics industry as a whole,

while other towns in Aragon and Catalonia led the way in tile making. Wares from Valencia were especially popular in Italy, traveling there via the Spanish island of Majorca. This is how the name "maiolica" came to be adopted, even though the style did not originate on Majorca and the island never had a significant practical association with tile production.

One of the most interesting craftsmen making maiolica tiles in Spain was an Italian called Francisco Niculoso who moved to Seville at the end of the fifteenth century and there introduced fine Italian glazes. His tile panels of religious subjects incorporated architectural settings drawn from classical antiquity, and his draftsmanship was crisp and assured. He portrayed different textures with graphic patterns such as crosshatching and stippling, drawn in minute detail, and he built up a great variety of vivid and subtle colors by layering one colored glaze over another. Not surprisingly, his work was acclaimed and popular, and he won many

Opposite A charming street fountain in Sintra, Portugal is a reminder of that country's extraordinary history of tile making, which resulted in almost every building imaginable being decorated with panels of azulejos.

prestigious commissions for altar frontals and panels for other prominent positions in the city's many religious and civic buildings.

Tile panels of this period varied from small compositions of six or eight tiles to magnificent walls constructed from several thousand. The exact area of the wall was measured out on the floor of the workshop, allowing for doors and windows and any other architectural features. Biscuit-fired tiles coated with plain white tin glaze were then laid on to this space and decorated by the master tile maker. They were numbered or carefully recorded on a plan of allocation before being removed for firing. Once the tiles were made, the huge mural was usually installed by a mason who attached them to the wall with plaster in the correct formation.

Spain's neighbor Portugal also had a rich tradition of tin-glazed decorated wall tiles. In the course of the fifteenth and sixteenth centuries, small tiles made in geometric shapes and known as *alicatados* were superseded by larger tiles which made covering whole walls a quicker and technically easier task. These tiles began to be produced in Lisbon in the second half of the sixteenth century, and were given the name *azulejos*, from the Arab word for ceramic mosaic, *zuleija*. Thus began one of Europe's most outstanding tile traditions.

For centuries, Portuguese architecture had gained much of its effect from applied decoration, using decorative painting, gilding, wood carving and inlaid marbles to embellish the surfaces of buildings, both inside and out. The discovery of the potential of tiled surfaces gave Portuguese craftsmen a new and refreshing outlet for their talents. They developed a wonderfully free and creative style, painting panels with vigorous draftsmanship and incorporating designs and images from a mass of sources. These panels covered whole walls, even whole rooms, and were extensively used outdoors on terraces and in gardens.

LEFT Shades of blue against antique off-white create a striking graphic design on these tiles decorating the cloister of the church of Sao Gonci.

OPPOSITE A magnificent interior in the former convent of Santa Rosa at Puebla, Mexico. The tiles have been used to cover every available surface, including the vaulted ceiling, to create a visual impact.

Popular prints from France and Italy, religious stories and themes, textile designs, even Hindu motifs drawn from imported Indian calicoes, were all represented figuratively on the Portuguese tiles, while abstract decoration took the form of energetically robust curling patterns and borders. Ironically, the tiles developed this richness and originality only when the industry became centered on smaller towns and workshops in the wake of the country's political and economic decline in the late sixteenth century. Economic recovery came at the end of the seventeenth century, and with it a mass of commissions for palaces, houses and gardens.

Brazilian gold played an important part in the dynamism of Portugal's tile industry in the eighteenth century, which benefited from the sumptuous wealth of the ruling and mercantile classes and their corresponding desire for magnificent display. Tiled rooms became increasingly flamboyant, opening up wall space visually with broad landscapes and daring use of perspective. During this period, blue and white tiled decoration was especially popular, but renewed interest in a wider palette returned towards the middle of the century. All the styles that dominated the arts in Europe in following centuries, through the baroque, rococo and neoclassical periods, were reflected in Portugal's breathtaking *azulejos*.

In Italy, meanwhile, maiolica reached equally magnificent heights of achievement but in different spheres. The fine modeling and color of the maiolica sculptures and sculptural plaques made by the della Robbia family of Florence, showing

scenes in the life of the Holy Family and other biblical subjects, deserve comparison with the greatest fine art of Renaissance Italy. The della Robbias also made decorated tiles, but this was not the work for which they were best known.

Italy differed from Spain and Portugal in that tiles were primarily, though not exclusively, used on floors rather than on walls and ceilings. The brilliant effect of the most magnificent of these tiled floors, laid in wealthy churches, homes and other buildings, owes as much to the inventive combination of different-shaped tiles (reminiscent in some cases of English medieval tile mosaics) as to the lively decoration painted on to them with colored tin glazes.

Many of the floors incorporated hexagonal lozenges, either used exclusively or in combination with other shapes. A floor in the Giustiniani Chapel in Venice groups lozenges around square tiles, with triangles in each group, to form a larger

square. A particularly beautiful floor at San Giminiano has six lozenges painted with leaves and lemons on a white background, grouped around a regular hexagon of pale blue with a rosette at its center painted in manganese on white. The tile border of this floor has cornucopias spilling fruit, verdant green leaves and yellow palms.

In Rome, the Vatican Palace has an intriguing and beautiful floor consisting entirely of diamond-shaped tiles radiating in star-like groups of six from a grid of points, and the cathedral in Siena has an even simpler but equally effective floor composed entirely of regular triangles, each with a painted rope border and yellow crescent on blue in the center. More elaborate floors incorporated circular tiles, around which others fitted either in a regular grid of bars framing squares, or in a complicated pattern of curved pieces which must have severely taxed the ingenuity of the designer and tile makers. At Deruta, one of the Italian cities at the forefront of maiolica production along with Florence, Siena, Casteldurante, Perugia and, above all, Faenza, one special floor is covered with tiles of two interlocking shapes familiar from Islamic tile art. Eight-pointed stars are linked with crosses, each arm of the cross ending in a point. These Islamic echoes notwithstanding, the decoration is entirely Christian, with a saint or *putto* in the center of each star. These and some of the floors incorporating circles (reminiscent of English medieval floors) are a reminder of the way in which patterns recur throughout the history and geography of tile making as new designers and craft tilers try out familiar styles.

In countries across Europe in the sixteenth century, Italian maiolica tiles were hugely popular among those who could afford them, a fact not surprising considering their beauty and vitality. The enthusiasm led to most countries setting up their own industries. In France one of the Rouen potteries was led by a craftsman who had worked with Girolamo della Robbia, and in Paris the modern formal gardens of the Tuileries mark the spot where a tile-works factory stood until 1664; now all that remains is the name. Industries were also founded in Austria, Germany and—most significantly, as the next chapter demonstrates—Antwerp in what was then the Netherlands.

DUTCH AND ENGLISH
DELFT

OPPOSITE Hundreds of similar tiles (no two identical) showing a tree with a figure or figures alongside have been used in rows to line this magnificent interior. To the right of the doorway the tree is on the left of each tile, to the left the tree is on the right. In the far room this pattern is reversed. The repetition creates a rhythmic effect that is restful and appealing.

MODERN HOLLAND is only a fraction of the size of the country that was known as the Netherlands when tin-glazed ware began to be made there. In the early sixteenth century, the Netherlands included today's Belgium and the Belgian town of Antwerp. Links between the Netherlands and southern Europe were strong, since the Netherlands was part of the Holy Roman Empire, ruled over in the sixteenth century by Spanish kings. Two types of tile were made there for use on floors: one was lead-glazed earthenware produced by modest local craftsmen. The other was maiolica, made by the aristocrats of the ceramics industry, Italian craftsmen like Guido Andries, who emigrated from Casteldurante to Antwerp in the sixteenth century and introduced their sophisticated techniques of preparing, glazing and decorating tiles.

At this time even lead-glazed earthenware tile floors were laid only in the homes of wealthy subjects, in public buildings and by the church. Maiolica floor tiles, which were more expensive and much less durable, were the province of only a small number of churches and nobles of great wealth, who enjoyed them for their novelty as much as for their beauty. Their appearance was identical to the maiolica discussed in the previous chapter: brightly and vigorously painted decoration, usually in blue, yellow, green and manganese, on the sparkling white ground that tin glaze provided.

BELOW The Dutch tiles of around 1580 show the connection between maiolica and delft, not only in their colors but also in the strong lines of their decoration.

47

LEFT A handsome decorated jar has been wittily placed in a corner, in front of tiled panels showing handsome decorated jars, these containing flower displays.

OPPOSITE An interior in the Low Countries showing tiles lining the walls. When picture tiles are used over a large area, the corner motifs combine to make a strong contribution to the overall effect.

Towards the end of the sixteenth century there was an explosion in demand for tin-glazed tiles. The popularity of maiolica had grown so much in previous decades that craftsmen who were originally involved in producing lead-glazed tiles switched to tin glazes, without at first changing their decorative style. Existing workshops were therefore in a position to satisfy this demand to some extent, but numerous new factories opened.

Two important reasons for the rising demand for tiles were an enormous expansion in the population, and increased prosperity, especially among a fast-growing middle class. The population increase was the result of political upheaval in response to rule from Spain, taxation without representation, and suppression of Protestantism by the Roman Catholic King. The northern part of the Netherlands was a Protestant stronghold and finally became a separate state, the United Provinces of the Netherlands. In the meantime, a steady flow of people had moved from the Roman Catholic south to the safety and sympathetic environment offered by the north. Among them were many wealthy Protestant families, professionals and entrepreneurs, together with craftsmen such as sophisticated Antwerp tile makers.

The money and spirit of enterprise these people brought with them gave an extra boost to the successful and growing economy. Natives of neighboring Germany were also attracted to the Netherlands and further swelled the population. Prosperity was capped by the establishment of the Dutch East India Company in the early years of the seventeenth century. This company imported the goods that, more than anything, influenced the style of tiles and ceramics that has made Holland perennially famous—Chinese porcelain decorated in blue and white.

Another factor in the huge growth in demand for tin-glazed tiles at the end of the sixteenth century was interior fashion.

LEFT Tiles of similar design, with almost identical church towers, showing the color differences of both pattern and background created by the use of different glazes.

Maiolica tiles were far from ideal as a floor covering since the glaze and decoration were easily damaged underfoot. But when attached to the wall, their delicacy ceased to be a problem. In about 1580, maiolica wall tiles were introduced to the market and proved a popular and commercial success. National prosperity meant that a large number of people could afford them. And in practical as well as decorative terms they transformed the inside of the home. Moreover, in the western Netherlands and coastal regions, around the wealth-generating ports and trading posts (where much of the population growth in the later sixteenth and first half of the seventeenth centuries was concentrated), the ground level was more often than not below the water table and houses were consequently wringing wet, especially where walls met floors. At that time, exterior walls were without insulation or protective cavities, and indoor walls were plastered and given a coat of whitewash. This flaked, and efflorescence meant that it brushed off on anything that touched it, which in passages and narrow parts of the house meant the clothing of the inhabitants.

It soon became apparent that tin-glazed wall tiles were both waterproof and easy to maintain. They were therefore quickly adopted to overcome damp problems by being used as skirting or baseboards in rooms, and covering larger areas of wall in hallways and corridors. Tiles were also used in and around the house's fireplace, of which there was usually one large one with a high mantelpiece in the room that doubled as a kitchen and living room at the back of the ground floor. The wall

LEFT Modern delft tiles
decorated with figures
of Saracens, the
Moorish warriors
probably seen by
potters who traveled
north to Rotterdam in
about 1610.

immediately to each side of the fireplace might also be tiled to protect it from grease and soot as well as making it an attractive feature of a room.

One of the most popular designs of this period, called *kwadraattegel*, had a square drawn within the square of the tile, but upended to form a diamond shape. This frame was filled with a picture, of an animal or flower vase for example (the latter pattern was so popular it was produced by at least thirty tile works). The corners outside the diamond were filled with stylized leaves painted in blue and white—the forerunner of the corner decoration on delft tiles. Another popular design incorporated pomegranates, also known as orange apples, which could be interpreted as referring to the House of Orange. This noble family is today the Dutch royal family, and provided Great Britain with its late-seventeenth-century King William III, spouse of Queen Mary, last reigning monarch of the House of Stuart.

The tiles were still recognizably maiolica, painted in several colors including a lively orange-yellow. But as the seventeenth century progressed, this palette was superseded by a more restrained one—the instantly recognizable blue and white that we associate with Dutch ceramics. The Dutch East India Company's supply of Chinese porcelain was not the only significant influence on this development. Fashions in clothing and interior decoration were veering towards the sober and subdued—a mood which fitted the restraint of a simple blue and white palette exactly.

Decoration on tiles became quieter: the busy diamond shape was frequently replaced by a cool circle containing a figure or figurative scene; and the decoration in the corners was reduced to an elegant, spidery motif in place of the bold and heavy leaves fashionable in former times. This trend towards the restrained can also be seen in the fine art of the time, with Rembrandt demonstrating and exploiting to the full the

OPPOSITE AND RIGHT Delft
panels showing (left)
various figures, scenes
and sea creatures and
(right) simple landscapes
with a tree. Each tile has
a tiny graphic motif in
each corner.

dramatic potential of black clothing and a near-monochrome
treatment of light and color.

Besides the impact Chinese porcelain had on the decoration
of tiles, it was responsible for at least three other effects on the
ceramics industry. The imports included no tiles but great
quantities of other ceramics. Rather than compete, the
majority of factories in the Netherlands (of which there were
now a great number) chose to leave aside ceramic production
to concentrate on tile making. In the town of Delft itself, two
factories decided not to be defeated by the porcelain imports,
but to try and beat the Chinese at their own game. They
refined their materials and technique in order to produce
ceramics which could compare with the fineness, smoothness
and whiteness of Chinese porcelain. In the middle of the
seventeenth century these technical advances were transferred
to tile making, and resulted in thinner, lighter tiles.

In 1650, a dramatic event overtook the Dutch ceramics
industry. Civil war in China suddenly extinguished the trade
in Chinese porcelain. The factories in Delft that had improved
their technique and successfully imitated the Chinese wares
stepped into the breach and were flooded with orders. Other
factories in the town quickly began production, and thus
began the boom that resulted in the name delft being
associated with all Dutch tiles and ceramics, and even
with English ceramics produced in the same style. The town
did not enjoy a monopoly, however. Other centers of
ceramic—particularly tile—production existed in Rotterdam,
Harlingen and Makkum.

LEFT Windmills are, not surprisingly, a recurring theme in the decoration of Delft tiles, though the type and construction of the windmills depicted varies.

Over the next fifty years, decoration on tiles generally became sparser, though the market for more highly-decorated tiles did not disappear completely. Also during this period, more customers came from the country and fewer from the towns, where the fashion in interior decoration had once again changed. Among the middle classes, fabric and leather took over from tiles, which were relegated to cellars and the kitchen (now frequently a separate room from the main living room).

Foreign customers, meanwhile, continued to import Dutch tiles as well as making their own imitations, and delftware held a steady place in markets across the world well into the nineteenth century and beyond. There was hardly a part of the civilized world into which delft tiles were not imported, including North and South America (especially Brazil with its long connection with Holland and Portugal) as well as European countries, of which Denmark and Germany were especially enthusiastic importers.

The range of subjects painted in a charmingly free and fresh style on delft tiles was huge, including flowers, animals, the human face (frequently of a well-known person), landscapes, seascapes, everyday life—including people's trades and occupations—and groupings of human figures. The latter often referred directly to a biblical episode; some of these were specifically Roman Catholic, such as scenes from the life of the Virgin, and were exported to Spain and Portugal. The sea played an important part in Dutch life, and seascapes were therefore extremely popular. Ships on tiles were sometimes portraits of specific vessels; other maritime subjects such as sea battles, whaling and the departure of Prince William of Orange to England in 1688, were also featured.

Among the most interesting subjects of decoration on Dutch tiles were children's games, which revealed a great deal, not only about the pastimes of childhood over several centuries, but also about society and religion of the period.

RIGHT Childhood games are another subject dear to the designers of delft tiles. Below is an antique tile showing children's ball games; above are modern delft tiles showing rope skipping, hoop rolling and stilts.

Some tiles, for example, made moral points such as warning against pretentiousness (hobby-horse riding) and about the transitory nature of temporal life (blowing bubbles). Others showed cherubs indulging in the same games enjoyed by their earthly siblings, such as rolling the hoop. Some games are no longer played today (flying live birds with a cord tied to one leg), while others like golf and kite-flying are still instantly recognizable. It is interesting that while tiles showing children (and indeed adults) playing games were hugely popular in the Netherlands as well as abroad in countries that imported Dutch tiles, they were rarely made by the tile industries that were established abroad as a result of the popularity of delftware.

In Britain, delftware tiles were imported in quantity and later manufactured in several cities. So fashionable were they that Henry VIII covered floors at Hampton Court Palace with Flemish tiles. A small tile making center in Norwich, founded in the 1560s by Jasper Andries from Antwerp, was the forerunner of thriving eighteenth-century delftware industries in London, Bristol, Liverpool and Glasgow.

The Bristol industry was founded in the 1680s and was technically competent by the 1730s. Tile makers from London, meanwhile, moved to Liverpool and made that city a tile making center of importance. It is no coincidence that these cities, and Glasgow, were all ports. New products and ideas were constantly flowing through them and were readily absorbed by indigenous craftsmen. Genuine Dutch delft tiles continued to be popular, partly because they were softer than

LEFT Antique Dutch delft tiles on the walls of a seventeenth century dairy. Tiles helped keep the place cool.

OPPOSITE A bathroom at Packwood House, Warwickshire, England, built and decorated by Graham Baron Ash between the World Wars. The walls are lined with delft tiles.

English ones. Known as "sandy backs," Dutch tiles could be cut to fit irregular shapes and spaces, which English ones could not with such ease.

English delft tiles gradually developed a style of their own, and the products of each city had their own distinctive elements. Bristol, for example, produced tiles with a unique type of border decoration, with one shade of white glaze painted delicately over the white background glaze of slightly different tone. This is known as *bianco-sopra-bianco* (white-on-white). Liverpool tiles often had polychrome decoration, while London tiles followed more closely the decoration of blue and white Dutch originals. The English tin glaze was very slightly blue or green because it had a higher lead content, whereas the basic white Dutch glaze contained more tin and was therefore whiter, but more likely to craze. It was also often less smooth and rich, while the English glaze was soft and glossy.

The Dutch delft industry survived and continues to produce to this day, but the English industry was short-lived in contrast. The first blow to it was struck by two men, John Sadler and Guy Green, who developed a new method of transfer printing, the precursor of nineteenth-century industrial methods of mass-producing decorated tiles. Tin-glazed ceramics of all types were also challenged in the eighteenth century by new products from the potteries of men such as Josiah Spode and Josiah Wedgwood, whose names are synonymous even today with high-quality stoneware of timeless design.

VICTORIAN TILES

THE VICTORIAN AGE is well known as a period of inventiveness and enthusiasm. It was characterized by innovative and eager use of advances in mechanization to create and promote a huge range of products that affected ordinary people's lives. Everything from railways crisscrossing nations and continents to the manufacture of buttons for clothing was touched by this passion. The motive was largely commercial, but success was not possible without a positive attitude towards change and progress—the attitude that new ideas were exciting. At the same time, this love affair with industrial mechanization displayed by some Victorians was balanced by another sort of enthusiasm, for philanthropy, public works such as sewers and healthy housing, and the improvement of the mind and quality of life through contact with art and man-made (as opposed to machine-made) crafts.

Nothing escaped industrialization, least of all the tile, which was produced in vast numbers. In previous periods of history the design of tiles generally developed in one particular, distinctive direction, a result of technical advances as much as the popularity of a particular visual style. In the Victorian period, the application of various industrial methods resulted in tile making taking off in a dozen different directions, its trails making quite as elaborate a pattern as the railways across Europe. Trying to keep

LEFT AND BELOW Encaustic tiles, including matching borders, continue to be made today.

59

ABOVE In Victorian England the authorities delighted in decorating public facilities with tiles. This is a detail of a drinking fountain built in 1868 near the Houses of Parliament in London.

track of the decorating methods, the range of subjects used in decoration, the technical advances and the companies who designed and made tiles induces a sense of confusion and euphoria. It was an exciting time for tile-making.

If it is possible to begin with only one man. The person who probably initiated the new age for tiles was the architect Augustus Welby Pugin (1815-52). His interest, ironically, was in the manufacture and decoration of tiles which recalled medieval England, rather than in the pursuit of industrialization. By looking backwards, he hoped to enrich the present, and in particular the churches and grand buildings he was commissioned to design or advise upon. Pugin was gifted and energetic, and achieved success as an architect at an early age. A convert to the Roman Catholic faith, he was passionate about the Christian significance of Gothic architecture in the Middle Ages.

Pugin adopted the Gothic style for the contemporary buildings he designed. His influence was enormous, his active years coinciding with the rapid increase in church-going and church building that followed the growth in urban populations caused by the industrial revolution. And he was not only concerned with the buildings; he involved himself with every detail of the furnishings of the interiors, as did later influential designers such as William Morris and Charles Rennie Mackintosh. Thus he designed not only the exterior detail of the Houses of Parliament at Westminster but also the hat stands and inkwells used by Members of Parliament and peers inside the building.

ABOVE These tiles were made with "plastic clay," in its wetter form, rather than drier clay dust. The design shows an interest in medieval tiles.

Tiled floors were the only appropriate floors, as far as Pugin was concerned, and the only appropriate tiles were, of course, earthenware, inlaid tiles in the medieval style. These were known in the Victorian period as "encaustic" tiles, and Pugin's passion for them prompted a contemporary to say: "Among the various objects occupying Pugin's attention, not one received a greater share than the revival of the manufacture of encaustic tiles." This commitment, combined with that of the tile manufacturer Herbert Minton, could be said to have laid the foundation of the massive Victorian tile industry.

In addition to the new churches that were being built, many existing churches were restored in the new enthusiasm for Gothic architecture. Considered ugly in the eighteenth century when cool classicism held sway, many medieval tiled floors had simply been boarded over and thus preserved, to be uncovered by the Victorians. Such floors, as well as those in public places like the Chapter House of Westminster Abbey,

provided models for the design of new encaustic tiles. Minton's firm led the way in their production.

Two years before Victoria came to the throne in 1837, Herbert Minton had bought up the molds, equipment and stock of an unsuccessful and disillusioned inventor, Samuel Wright. He also bought a share in the patent on Wright's invention, a mechanized method of manufacturing inlaid earthenware tiles. This method involved pressing so-called "plastic" clay into a mold at whose bottom was a raised pattern. The indentations left in the clay by the raised pattern were subsequently filled with liquid clay (called "slip") of a different color, resulting in a patterned tile very much in the style of medieval floor tiles.

The term "plastic" refers to what most people think of as ordinary clay—a natural material rather like solidified mud. The term is used to make a distinction between this method of tile production and the later method which took over from

SVMMER

OPPOSITE "Summer," a magnificent and detailed tile panel designed by the nineteenth-century artist Poynter and made by Minton, Campbell and Co. for the Dutch Kitchen.

RIGHT Part of a richly colored marble tiled floor at Osborne House on the Isle of Wight.

it and revolutionized tile production. It is known as the dust-pressing method. Minton bought a share in the patent for this in 1840, when it was being used by its inventor, Richard Prosser, to make buttons.

By taking clay dust and pressing it into a mold under tremendous force, it was possible to make tiles that presented few of the technical problems that arose in the plastic clay method. The clay dust had just enough moisture in it for it to stick together when compressed in the mold, but needed very little time to dry before being ready for firing. By the end of Victoria's reign, few tiles were made by any other method. In 1844 Wright's patent came up for renewal and was bought by Minton in partnership with another tile manufacturing company, G. Bar & Fleming St. John.

Tile production became a source of fascination to the highest in the land as well as to foreign dignitaries. In the previous year, Queen Victoria's husband, Prince Albert,

witnessed a demonstration given by Minton's chief engineer at a soirée held by the Marquess of Northampton. Also present were the Duke of Wellington, the Prime Minister, Sir Robert Peel, over two dozen foreign princes and, also of great importance considering their huge potential for patronage, several bishops. Prince Albert was deeply interested, and the following year Minton was commissioned to tile the spacious corridor being built by Thomas Cubitt to connect the main block and the pavilion of Osborne House, Queen Victoria's summer family home on the Isle of Wight.

Minton's success was assured. The Minton Hollins catalogue of 1881 (by which time the company had split into several parts, of which Minton Hollins was the main tile manufacturer) gave a long list of prestigious commissions fulfilled. Not only does the list make entertaining reading; it also reveals the range of structures and the extent of overseas orders that Minton supplied. The list includes: "The Royal

LEFT The owners of the Warrington Hotel in Maida Vale, London, invested in elaborate molded and glazed tiles for the outside of the building, here depicting acanthus leaves, a lion's head and oak leaves with acorns.

Palaces of Windsor, Osborne, Clarence House, Sandringham and Marlborough House; the Imperial Palace of the Emperor of Germany; the Palace and State Yachts of the Sultan of Turkey; the Royal Residence of Prince Dhuleep Singh; the Houses of Parliament, Westminster; the New Foreign Offices; the New Government Buildings in India and Australia; the South Kensington Museum; the Albert Hall; the Senior and Junior Carlton Clubs; the Cathedrals of Ely, Lincoln, Lichfield, Gloucester, Westminster, Wells, Glasgow, Armagh, St. Giles' Edinburgh, Dunblane and Sydney (New South Wales); the New Capitol of Washington (U.S.A.); the Town Halls of Liverpool, Leeds, Rochdale, Bolton, etc.; the Municipal Buildings of Birmingham and Liverpool; and many of the principal Ducal Mansions, Government Buildings, Churches and Public Institutions of Great Britain, etc." That last "etc." is a delightful ending which seems to say, "And every other type of important building you care to mention."

From the greatest building to the smallest, tiles quickly became a necessary element, more than just a decorative detail. The Victorian period, especially the 1880s and 1890s, saw a huge amount of speculative building in the suburbs of cities. Street upon street of houses for workers of every rank sprang up—terraced and semidetached houses largely of great charm which are still coveted homes today. Hardly one was without a tiled path, porch, hallway or passage, at the very least. Tiles were used almost as extensively on walls as on floors. In small houses the spaces involved were a fraction of the areas in a palace, church or town hall, and it was the builder rather than an architect, owner or dignitary who chose the tiles to be laid. For these customers, the geometric tile was introduced.

Instead of the pattern being inlaid into square tiles, it was constructed *in situ* from separate tiles of geometric shape, each one a different color, which fitted together like the pieces of a puzzle into any pattern the builder or owner cared to invent.

BELOW A paved path leading to the front door of a Victorian house in Hammersmith, London. Small geometric tiles like these were chosen from a catalog and assembled in any design you wanted.

The method is reminiscent of medieval tile "mosaic," although the fifteenth-century monk could not, of course, pick his pieces from a catalog. The choice of shapes was now huge: a page from the Campbell Tile Company catalog of 1885 shows 109 different, compatible tiles with straight and curved edges, cut from a six-inch square. Geometric tiles could be and were used in conjunction with inlaid encaustic tiles on a single floor, as can be seen in many parish churches.

It was not only homes, palaces and government buildings that were tiled. The inside and outside of shops, offices, workshops, libraries, public lavatories, railway stations and underground stations were faced with tiles, often incorporating the name of the proprietor or place. Laws governing building standards were introduced, and advances in science and attitudes towards medical care also played a part in promoting a more positive attitude towards hygiene than had previously existed. Hospitals and food shops like butchers and fishmongers embraced the glazed tile as the ideal hygienic wall and floor covering. The result was magnificent interiors like Harrods' food halls in London (a late-Victorian creation, completed in 1901) designed by W. J. Neatby for the firm of Doulton. Just as medieval church floors had been covered up when out of fashion, so the Harrods food halls were hidden behind twentieth-century lowered ceilings and streamlined cladding, to be rediscovered and restored to their full glory in the late 1980s.

The most popular method of decorating Victorian tiles was by transfer printing, a technique inherited from Sadler's

65

RIGHT No. 46 is fortunate to be decorated with this charming tile panel showing Ye Early Mower taking a rest from his labors and enjoying a refreshing drink from a small barrel.

OPPOSITE A wash stand with tiled splashback in one of the rooms at the splendid granite Castle Drogo in Devon, built by Sir Edwin Lutyens for the Drewe family between 1910 and 1930.

eighteenth-century printing system. This involved inking the decoration on to a thin piece of paper, either from an engraved metal plate or from a lithographic stone, using oil-based inks. The tissue was then laid on a once-fired biscuit tile with the ink next to the clay, rubbed, and soaked off in water. The design would then be left on the tile. A low-temperature firing fixed the inks before a final glaze was added and the tile was fired once again. Extra color could be hand-painted over the transfer decoration either after or, more usually, before this final glaze. Transfer engravings produced decoration with precise lines; lithographs were better for designs with solid areas of color.

Transfer printing was just one of many methods of decoration with which the manufacturers of wall tiles experimented. Painting by hand was the freest, though this was sometimes preceded by "pouncing" the outlines of a design through tiny holes in paper with powdered charcoal. Another type of decoration, tube lining, involved squeezing thin lines of clay on to the tile, like cake icing, and filling the separate sections thus created on the surface with glazes of different colors. Relief tiles had the subject impressed into the clay so that the glaze pooled in the deeper areas, making a darker color, while shallower areas showed a much paler shade of the glaze color. The most modern decorative technique was photographic and used mostly to transfer shallow relief likenesses of famous people onto wall tiles.

Pâte sur pâte also worked on a similar principle to relief decoration, but the thicker areas of glaze were built up

OPPOSITE This delightful tile surround is found in the night nursery at Wightwick Manor near Wolverhampton. The house was begun in 1887 and decorated using the period's best designers, including work by William Morris.

LEFT Contemporary tiles inspired by designs of the Arts and Crafts period.

gradually on the flat tile by being painted on by hand, a painstaking process. By comparison, *sgraffito* was a fairly primitive decorative method. Coats of contrasting slip were laid on the tile and the design scratched through the upper layer or layers, revealing the color beneath. Aerography was a little-used method of spraying glaze through a stencil onto the tile surface, which resulted in flat areas of color which can be seen on close examination to have a speckled quality and sometimes a slight blurring of the edges.

Lists and analyses of the subjects shown on Victorian tiles fill whole books—almost nothing escaped. Flowers were immensely popular on tiles, as in every branch of the applied arts in the Victorian era. They appeared in realistic form, flattened and stylized in more schematic form, incorporated into geometric patterns, and in tiles with a so-called "Persian" theme. Tiles were even transfer printed to imitate embroidery of flowers on canvas. Following on from flowers were leaves, fruit, birds, animals (local and exotic), insects, fish, landscapes, the elements, the seasons and the days of the week.

A large number of designs incorporated the human figure, and many of these referred to works of literature. Characters from popular fiction and contemporary poetry were balanced by mythological and Shakespearean heroes and heroines. Religious subjects were popular, and mottoes, such as "Waste Not Want Not," which were probably incorporated into the kitchen tiling as admonishment to the servant or housewife. For children there were cherubs, fairies, songs and nursery rhymes, with some of the period's most celebrated illustrators, such as Kate Greenaway and Walter Crane, contributing designs. Many accomplished artists, whose names are not as famous as these, worked for the tile manufacturers, and as a result much tile decoration was lively and charming.

Painted panels, the largest incorporating dozens of tiles, decorated shops with scenes considered appropriate to the

LEFT Minton, the tile company that made this design during the nineteenth century, was one of the most prolific and successful tile manufacturing enterprises of the period.

goods or food being sold—cows or a bull in a landscape for a butcher's shop, for example. And hospitals, especially children's wards, were similarly decorated but with scenes calculated to cheer the patient, such as nursery rhymes and lush pastorals. Sporting scenes on panels and individual tiles ranged from the heat of the chase to the game of croquet played on smooth lawns, and even chess. Figures in these were as likely to be in medieval as modern dress. The trades were a popular subject, as was the idyllic portrayal of activities connected with agriculture. Food and meals decorated many tiles, as did associated mottoes and homilies such as "Eat thy food with a thankful heart," and "A little pudding adds to the repast."

Machine-based industrial production of tiles made this huge choice available to millions of people. William Morris and his followers, on the other hand, proposed that the machine could not be used to produce any object of true artistic merit. The irony that this position made art elitist by putting it beyond the means of most ordinary people was not lost on him and he later softened this view to allow the machine to be a tool in the artist's hand. Today he is famous primarily as a designer of timeless wallpapers which are still in production. In his own age he was a prominent man of ideas. His views provided leadership for many artists and craftsmen who found mechanization unsympathetic or incompatible with their work.

The movement he led away from machine production was known as "Arts and Crafts." In another interesting twist in the history of tiles, Arts and Crafts designs and ideas in general were influential in Holland. Dutch methods of production were small scale and craftsman based, rather than large-scale industrial, so the Dutch tile industry was fertile ground on which Morris's ideas thrived. Many Dutch tiles of the period could be mistaken at first glance for Morris creations.

LEFT A tile designed by the brilliant William De Morgan and found in the billiard room of Wightwick Manor, Wolverhampton, England.

Tiles that British Arts and Crafts artists decorated were not wholly successful, either technically or decoratively, and it was left to one particular artist, William De Morgan, to carry the banner into the world of ceramics. Trained as a painter, De Morgan came to tile-making via involvement with Morris and experiments with stained glass. He was a single-minded genius whose designs are among the finest artistic creations of the Victorian age but whose business acumen was almost nil. He ended his life as a successful novelist, still producing magnificent designs but forced by ill health to live abroad, divorced from his (now defunct) ceramic works in London.

William De Morgan produced expensive tiles with wonderfully dynamic and colorful designs. His most frequent subjects were plants and flowers, exotic and mythical birds and beasts, and ships with billowing sails, often boldly decorated, skimming across choppy seas peopled with porpoises. The forms are bursting with energy, almost too much so to be contained by the edges of the tile. Any spare space around the creatures is almost invariably filled with semi-abstract tufts of grass, sprigs of vegetation or swirling leaves, always exquisitely drawn and taking nothing away from the central figures.

De Morgan, like other Arts and Crafts artists, was strongly influenced by the designs and colors of Islamic tiles. His favorite palettes included either strong blues and greens familiar from Iznik work, or a distinctive rich red luster. The colors stand out brilliantly against the strong white glaze that De Morgan applied to blank biscuit tiles made from plastic rather than dust clay.

Although Arts and Crafts designers—apart from De Morgan—may not have been adept at making or decorating tiles, they used tiles enthusiastically in an applied context. In particular they incorporated them into pieces of furniture, sometimes ordering them from Holland or Turkey for the purpose. Arts and Crafts architects like Philip Webb and

OPPOSITE A sunflower tile design by William De Morgan, typical in the assured draftsmanship and sensual curls of its leaves.

LEFT The Victorians used tiles everywhere they could; here, a window box in Chelsea, London, inhabited at that time by artists and bohemians, is decorated with tiles showing crocuses, guaranteeing flowers all year round.

Richard Norman Shaw faced buildings with terra-cotta tiles in the age-old vernacular method of tile-hanging, which they revived and juxtaposed with brickwork, stone, half-timbering and plaster.

An offshoot of the British tile industry, and the Victorian era's mania for huge international exhibitions of industrial and "artistic" products, was the American tile industry. At first, British companies dominated the American scene, employing agents to promote and sell their tiles. Companies such as Minton Hollins staged splendid displays at shows like the World of Science, Art and Industry in New York in 1853. The American authorities encouraged British craftsmen and technical experts to emigrate to a more prosperous life and bring their expertise to the youthful industries of the New World. As a result, in the last three decades of the nineteenth century companies producing tiles indigenous to the United States sprang up across the breadth of the country, and as often as not failed within years. This rapid turnover in companies means that a history of American tiles threatens to read like little more than a list of names. In fact the industry had a distinctive character of its own that distinguished it from its British parent.

Tiles were never as common a feature of Victorian architecture in America as they were in Europe; also, the transfer printing technique was never as popular as in Britain. The American tile industry was more preoccupied with hand-made and hand-finished "artistic" tiles than mass-produced printed ones. Edwin Atlee Barber, author and commentator on the ceramics industry of the United States, observed that "It is to the broad extension of the Arts and Crafts movement that we should look for the best results in artistic development in this country." Tile making attracted the enthusiastic attention of artists and craftsmen as well as industrialists, and one result of this enthusiasm was the Tile Club, established in 1877. In New York on Wednesday evenings over a period of ten years, a group of artists entertained themselves by decorating tiles in the studio of one or another member. Perhaps the most famous members were the painter Winslow Homer and the architect Stanford White. It seems that as much time was spent on cheerful conversation and exchange of anecdotes as on artistic endeavor, but the growing membership of the club and its decade of existence bear witness to the general interest in tiles in America. The industry survived until the depression of the 1930s dealt it a final blow.

THE TWENTIETH CENTURY

WHEN THE TWENTIETH CENTURY DAWNED, Victoria was still on the throne of England. Interiors looked Victorian, and had done so for decades. A hundred years later, not only is the look of people's homes radically different, but the rate of change in interior fashion is much quicker. This new state of affairs was launched in Britain by the Festival of Britain in 1951, which heralded a modern, postwar, colorful, ration-free era. Later it was promoted by the arrival of DIY as a new leisure pastime and an industry. Other factors were an increasing number of full-color home interest magazines which found a ready market, and a preoccupation in all the media with the concept of "lifestyle," of which the home is an important part.

Three main themes or categories which divided the production and appearance of tiles at the beginning of the twentieth century still exist, perhaps even more strongly, almost a hundred years later. These are: industrial mass-production; semimechanized or smaller-scale industrial, hand-finished or craft production; and individual tiles and tile panels, hand-made or hand-decorated by skilled artists and craftspeople working alone or in very small groups.

As at the end of the nineteenth century, the great majority of tiles made in Britain at the end of the twentieth century are the result of industrial

OPPOSITE A bold design of green and blue leaves along the edges of hexagonal tiles on the floor of an early twentieth-century French bathroom.

ABOVE Relief tiles showing a cockerel (left) and turkey (right) are examples of the variety of tile produced by craftspeople today; these are by Sebastian John and Odette Wells.

75

LE PNEU
MICHELIN
BOIT L'OBSTACLE

PARIS-VIENNE
1902

BUCQUET sur WERNER

LEFT The exterior of the Michelin Building in Fulham, London, is decorated with tile panels including this one, showing Bucquet riding a Werner motorcycle in the 1902 Paris to Vienna race. Made by Gilardoni Fils et Cie of Paris in 1908–1910.

OPPOSITE This tile panel in the children's hospital at Paddington Green, London, was designed to cheer up ailing children and remind them of happier times.

mass-production and fall into the first category. Victorian tiles produced in this manner, however, have a strength of character, a variety, and a charm that most of today's bland, timid designs lack. Some Victorian industrially-produced tiles were hand-colored, which gave them an element of individuality. Today, richness of design and texture, energy and innovation are to be found not in tiles offered by the big industrial companies, but in the creations of an increasing number of individual craftspeople, who fall into the third category of producers.

These artist-designers are supported by a handful of small manufacturers and, since the early 1980s, by a few committed retailers. The latter also import craft tiles which are mechanically produced in smaller or larger quantities and are hand-finished or decorated. These tiles have usually been designed by artists, who may also be involved in the production process, and who are often continuing a local

tradition of tile production and decoration which has existed for many decades or even centuries. Colorful hand-painted tiles from Spain and Mexico are examples of these, as are blue and white tiles made in the delft style in Britain and elsewhere. Hand-finished and hand-decorated tiles have a special quality, often a slight roughness of finish and always a sense of individuality, which the smooth, seamlessly repetitive mass-produced tiles do not, and they fall into the second category. A century or more ago, this would have included work by William De Morgan and the Arts and Crafts artists following the ideas of William Morris.

This transfer of creativity and interest away from the industrial, towards the individual, can be charted through the events and styles of each decade of the twentieth century. The first of the century's styles, whose sinuous lines and curving flower and plant forms flow through from the Victorian period, is art nouveau. Though industrially produced, some of

76

the tiles decorated in the art nouveau style have a freshness and comparative simplicity, in their use both of line and of clear color, which look forward to the new century and away from the crowded detail and moody colors of Victorian style.

By the time art nouveau was the prevalent style, however, the heyday of tile production was over and declining demand caused the closure of many tile factories. In 1914, the onset of the First World War in Europe dealt a near-fatal blow to an industry which was in decline after enlivening domestic, civic and commercial architecture and interiors for generations of Europeans and Americans.

Between the First and Second World Wars, the prevalent styles in architecture and interiors were modernism and art deco, both of which demanded exactly the clean lines and hard surfaces which tiles provided. Modernism demanded that buildings and rooms be uncompromisingly of-the-moment, uncluttered by frills and ornamentation, with straight or archly curving lines and smooth surfaces. Tiles were decorated with geometric motifs or were plain, in colors like white, black, soft emerald green or pinky-beige, and were arranged in flat bands of color or in geometric patterns. An exception was the work of the Omega Workshop artists, amongst them Vanessa Bell and Duncan Grant. These artists, based in Bloomsbury in London, produced flamboyant, hand-painted, colorful work including tiles, under the eye of the man who introduced London to the vibrant colors of Post-Impressionism, Roger Fry.

The interwar period was not long enough or robust enough, however, commercially or in terms of design, to foster a new tile industry, and war intervened once again to suppress all but the essential industries. A tile industry emerged in Britain again after the war, mass-producing tiles for use in domestic bathrooms and kitchens, but it tended to use internal designers, who seemed barely to deserve the name. Kenneth

OPPOSITE The tiled panel on this storefront in Blois, France, is just one of the graphic elements which contribute to the appealing overall effect.

LEFT AND BELOW In the 1930s decorative details like these were common on the exterior of buildings. The cockerel in relief appears on the outside of the Hoover factory in West London.

Clark is a veteran tile artist who was a student at the Slade art school in London immediately after the war. He observed the situation in industry and found it depressing.

"The postwar period saw a dearth of new tile designs in industry. If what they were doing before the war could be sold then there was no incentive to change. A design policy as such was not a vital element of factory life. Staff designers if they existed were just another category of operative and were treated accordingly. The designer was often the head decorator who had some drawing skill and was able to adapt ideas suggested or supplied by the managing director or the sales representative. He was seldom trained as a designer or expected to be an innovator, but he was expected to churn out a continuous selection of designs until one caught the fancy of the person responsible for selecting what went into production. When, in the late '50s and '60s, design as a concept began to emerge, the designer was given more freedom—but sadly he could not come up with the goods having been so long creatively frustrated and imaginatively undeveloped. The results were rather pathetic."

This situation described by Kenneth Clark contrasts strongly with industry's enthusiasm for artist-designers a hundred years earlier. Leading artists and illustrators like Kate Greenaway, Randolph Caldecott and Walter Crane were then employed to design tiles. Even in the first years of the twentieth century, tile designs by the brilliant architect and artist C. F. A. Voysey were in production. This is not to say that modern artists do not make tiles. Throughout the

RIGHT Many artists have been attracted by the discipline of decorating tiles, not least among them Pablo Picasso.

80

Left A seat in Parc Güell in Barcelona, created by Antonio Gaudí and financed by the wealthy textile manufacturer Eusebi Güell. Gaudí used broken-up patterned and colored tiles on undulating surfaces with a freedom and boldness that are a revelation even today.

Below Gaudí has influenced generations of tile artists and architects, including the creators of this design in Los Angeles.

twentieth century, artists like Pablo Picasso, Salvador Dalí and Joan Miró have occasionally worked on tiles, but only for themselves or clients and not generally for industry.

The two great twentieth-century masters whose tile work is perhaps most original are Henri Matisse and Antonio Gaudí. In his old age, Matisse created a tile mural for a chapel in Vence, near where he lived in the South of France, using simple line drawings in black on gleaming white. The result, which shows the Virgin and Child and other biblical scenes, is thrillingly bold and direct. The gleaming hardness of the tiles and uncompromising black lines contrast dramatically with the strength of emotion both in the Virgin's protective figure and gentle embrace of the Christ child, and in the child's outstretched arms reaching to embrace us, as we look at him, and the whole world beyond us. Gaudí's work makes its impact in a completely different way. He used colored tiles on the surfaces of buildings and in other architectural ways, to

81

OPPOSITE This charming stenciled tile is part of a collection of twelve tiles known as The Farmyard Series. Designed by E E Strickland, they were manufactured by Carter & Co., circa 1930.

RIGHT A detail of the dynamic and appealing tile design outside a building in Bloomsbury, London, created in the 1960s using tin glazes and a limited palette of colors.

create a mosaic of rich tone and texture which is dazzling in its complexity. The Güell Park and other buildings in Barcelona, Spain represent some of his most glorious achievements using tiles.

One of the century's greatest potters, Bernard Leach, also made tiles occasionally. As with his pots, these show the influence of his childhood experiences of Japan and his lifelong interest in its art as well as the pottery of China and Korea. Shapes were startlingly simple and unadorned; decoration was graphic and hand-painted or incised, showing simple motifs of fish, trees or flowers, figures and landscapes. Colors were muted, with the color of the clay showing through subtle translucent glazes or complementing soft shades of green or blue. The tiles follow this pattern. Leach had many pupils, and his influence in the art schools was tremendous. Work in the Leach style and in terra-cotta was nick-named "ginger pottery" by younger artists who found it

drab and who reacted against it by using bright and strong colors. Followers of Leach, meanwhile, thought the use of color in such work garish and vulgar.

The current renaissance in tile design and production dates from the late 1970s. In the meantime, any colorful style and originality in tiles came largely from artists who had trained not as potters but as textile or graphic designers or as painters, like Kenneth Clark. He was primarily interested in color and dabbled in pottery one day a week while studying painting. But without any technical training in using glazes he had difficulty in making his colors stay on the vertical surfaces of pots. Instead, he turned to the horizontal tile, off which the glaze did not run so readily. In the 1960s the family firm, which he and his wife Ann founded, produced tiles with decoration in rich turquoise and burnt orange. They also found that customers wanted to use black tiles, mostly with red, turquoise or plain white.

Other rich colors like chocolate brown, dark green and purple were also popular. Many of these colors continued to be fashionable well into the 1970s, even when more muted colors came into vogue. As well as individual plain and motif tiles, the company produced border tiles decorated with fish, leaves and flowers, and tile panels decorated with the tube-line technique popular with the Victorians. The Victorian revival in the 1980s also prompted them to revive many designs by William De Morgan, and to create their own designs following his style.

Enthusiastic interest in tiles, among British art historians and amateur collectors as much as among artists working on tiles, resulted, in 1981, in the founding of the Tiles and Architectural Ceramics Society. As well as being a forum for the exchange of ideas and research, this group has become involved in conservation issues, helping protect historic tiles. An ever-increasing number of artists, meanwhile, produced tiles and tile panels in their own style, using a wide variety of techniques, derived from their own visual influences, so that the last decades of the nineteenth century show no one overall theme. Much of the work is bold, strong and colorful, produced for one-off selling exhibitions in art and craft galleries and for individual clients. Specialist tile shops also stock tiles by contemporary artists, though the financial rigors of business and the discipline and pressure of producing the required number of tiles of suitable quality mean that not all artist-tilers can cope with, or want to be involved with, the retail market.

Retailers have found that all types of fine tiles, including hand-finished terra-cotta, rough slate and smooth marble, and hand-decorated tiles of greater or lesser sophistication from all over the world, are immensely popular. The 1980s saw a boom in trade in these tiles, as homeowners were prosperous and channelled funds into beautifying their homes. Subsequent stagnation of the property market and the economies of western countries inevitably affected trade in tiles, but among artists there is no shortage of enthusiasm for their tilework and there are still plenty of commissions and customers. No recession can alter the basic attractions of well-designed, well-made tiles in the home, both in practical and in aesthetic terms.

SECTION 2:

TILES AT HOME

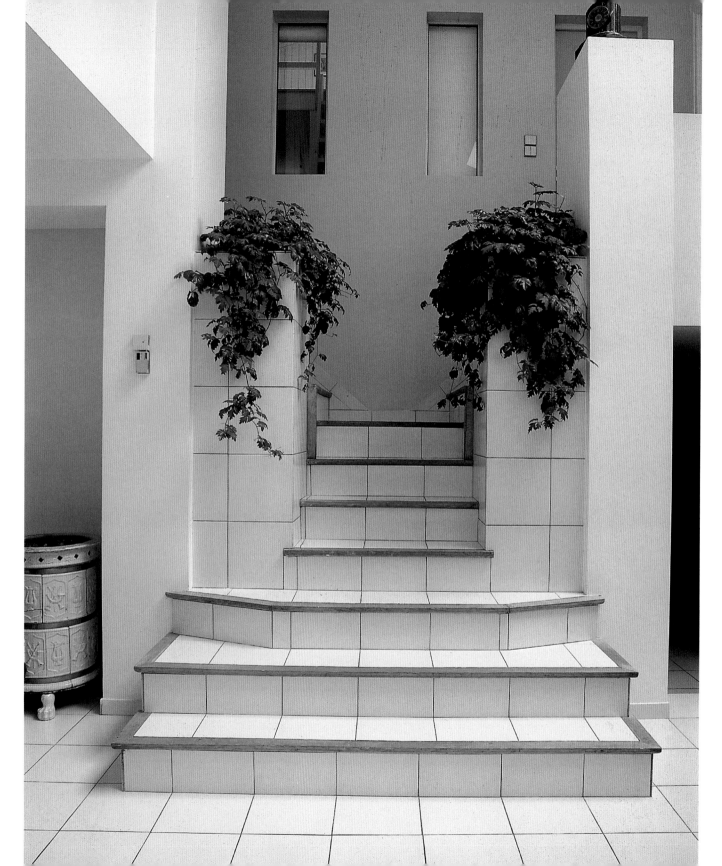

FLOORS
FUNCTION AND STYLE

OPPOSITE A staircase faced with white floor tiles with a contrasting grout. All-white has a severe, modernist look that is here softened by the wooden edging on the steps and a cascade of green foliage.

RIGHT African slate tiles in different sizes and shapes, each laid with a plain black square insert to create the traditional pattern.

THE USE OF TILES AS FLOOR COVERING has a long history, as previous chapters have shown. In the Western world during the twentieth century tiled floors never completely went out of use, but they did suffer periods of relative unpopularity. One such period, in which man-made synthetic floor coverings have been prominent, is undoubtedly coming to an end. The idea that natural materials are generally the most beautiful and the most pleasant to live with is now prevalent in all areas of home life, from clothing to wall paints and floor coverings.

Tiled floors fulfill this idea perfectly, at the same time offering a greater choice in terms of material, color and finish than was available in earlier centuries. Modern techniques make a wider range of tiles available for use on floors—for example, glazes and methods of firing which make ceramic tiles tougher than in previous centuries when they were considered suitable for wall decoration alone. Age-old methods of sealing and finishing tiled floors, such as sealing with boiled linseed oil and polishing with wax, have been joined by new approaches that can combine the best of old and new. Sealants and waxes that include synthetic components can provide labor-saving finishes on tiles laid in areas of the home that suffer especially hard wear—such as hallways, kitchens and children's playrooms.

OPPOSITE The home of artist Maria Foixa in Spain. The house is on different levels—the side of the stairs has been faced with antique tiles that are at eye level when you emerge from the room below.

Modern methods of transporting goods worldwide also mean that homeowners in Europe or America can equally easily choose brightly colored ceramic tiles made in their home country, or antique French terra-cotta tiles, or slate tiles from Africa. Many of the techniques used in making tiles have hardly changed in centuries and, together with the tiles themselves, have stood the test of time. Terra-cotta tiles not only do not deteriorate, they positively improve with use; as a patina builds up on the surface they become even more resilient to wear and tear, and their color becomes richer and more mellow.

The combined result of all these elements means simply that there is a tiled floor to suit every purpose and style of decoration in the contemporary home. The only limiting factors are practical—some particularly heavy tiles are not well suited for use on upstairs floors, for instance, and glazed tiles are inevitably more vulnerable to wear than unglazed ones—but practical considerations are also those that often make a tiled floor the best choice, and have done so since Roman times and before.

If you are in any doubt about whether to lay a tiled floor, the best approach is to consider the alternatives. Of all contemporary floor coverings, that which is blindly adopted more often than any other is carpet. Wall-to-wall carpeting certainly has attractions and an image of luxury, but it also has many disadvantages. In kitchens (and many people would say in bathrooms too) it is generally considered unhygienic. It wears out, quite quickly when it is of poor quality, and generally becomes increasingly tawdry in appearance as it wears. It is susceptible to marking, which makes it a nerve-racking commodity in any household with children or animals and totally unsuitable in areas where muddy boots and shoes are likely to tramp on it regularly. Moreover, it harbors dust and a variety of minute living organisms, some of which can cause distress to allergy and asthma sufferers.

Possible alternatives to carpet are linoleum, vinyl flooring and bare wooden floors. Linoleum is composed of natural materials including linseed oil and cork, which has many attractions and practical uses. But vinyl, like some other more recently invented man-made materials used in buildings, has come under suspicion of being less than healthy to people as it ages. There are reports that certain types of vinyl may give off gases over a long period of time. In purely aesthetic terms, vinyl is unpopular with people who prefer a real wooden or tiled floor to a synthetic floor covering which imitates those materials.

The most promising alternative is perhaps bare boards, which if sealed, treated or waxed, become less laborious to look after and can take on a color or finish. But wooden floors have their problems too. Drafts and dust can come up between the planks, small items can drop down the gaps, old boards are often crudely nailed down or cracked and broken and uneven. Noise can also be a problem with wooden floors, as they are usually suspended over a floor cavity, which causes them to act like a sounding board. Tiles are certainly not the quietest floor covering, but they are not necessarily as noisy as their

OPPOSITE A sumptuous courtyard interior, the fountain faced inside and out with small black and white tiles that find their echo in the classic black and white checkerboard patterned floor.

reputation suggests, since they are generally bedded on a solid floor, which dampens resonance.

Tiles also have a reputation for being cold and hard—certainly carpet would beat them on these scores, and would be more likely to break the fall of a fragile object dropped on it. But in countries like Holland, Germany, the Scandinavian nations and the U.S., where underfloor heating is not as unusual as it is in other parts of the Western world, tiles are considered a warm flooring. Laid on a solid base in which the underfloor heating pipes are buried, tiles are in direct contact with the source of heat and display what is called low thermal inertia. The porosity of the earthenware tile in particular means that it warms up quickly and retains heat.

People who have lived with extensive tiled floors, even without underfloor heating, leap to their defense when tiles are accused of being cold and hard. They declare that they are no colder than other hard floors, don't admit upward drafts like some old wooden floors, and in the case of materials like terracotta are positively warm and welcoming underfoot. In addition, they maintain that the aesthetic satisfaction and the practical advantages that a fine tiled floor gives far outweigh any supposed disadvantages. Tiles are water resistant, hygienic, practical, easy to clean, good looking, long lasting, and they positively improve with age.

Tiles can also be used in combination with other types of flooring. In a kitchen with a wooden floor and a wood stove, an area of floor in front of the stove can be tiled in a color complementary to the color of the enamel finish on the stove—yellow tiles against a pale blue stove, perhaps, and cherry red or deep blue against one that is racing green. In a living room or dining room with an open fire, you can tile the hearth in plain tiles and define its edge with a patterned border, or vice versa. If there is a stone or concrete hearth beneath the tiles, this will give them a solid base and they will simply need to be bedded on adhesive and grouted. If the floor beneath is wooden, lay the tiles on an adhesive compound designed to be elastic, to allow for any movement in the sprung floor beneath.

Deciding to have a tiled floor is just the beginning of the decision making process. The choice of tiles available is enormous and can be baffling. But as with any type of furnishing or decorating, the decision making can be helped by going back to basics and considering, in the case of tiles, the following factors:

MATERIAL • FINISH • COLOR

SIZE AND SHAPE • PATTERN

Tiles are made not only of fired clay but from various natural materials that are cut rather than fired to form tiles. These include stone, slate and marble. A clay tile can be earthenware or stoneware, which refers to the highest temperature at which it has been fired. Starting at about 1,100°F, porous earthenware undergoes a chemical change and fuses or vitrifies

OPPOSITE A modern home has been given an air of grandeur by the use of the traditional pattern of tiles laid with small black spacers filling in the corners of the white limestone octagons.

into stoneware. Stoneware is usually glazed, which guarantees that it has a hard, nonporous finish; earthenware is usually unglazed.

Earthenware tiles are generally known as terra cotta, but this term can be confusing because the word also means a warm color which could be described as brownish-pink or earthy red. Terra-cotta is a word of Latin origin which literally means "cooked earth" or "fired earth" and does not refer specifically to color. A terra-cotta tile can be terra-cotta colored, because the clay is that color before and after firing (called "red-firing" or "red-burning" clay), but it can also be a paler, more yellow shade. This may be because it has bleached in the sun over generations, or because it has been purposely bleached to make it paler, or because it is made from paler clay such as a type found in northern France. Today, a pale yellow color may also be due to chemical additives in the clay or some other form of manipulation such as blending.

Terra-cotta tiles today come from a number of countries, not only Italy. Spain, France and Mexico all make terra-cotta tiles for local consumption and export. Methods of production have changed little over the centuries. A certain amount of mechanization may have been introduced to the early stages, or to all stages, of production, and the supplier from whom you buy terra-cotta tiles should make it clear whether or not your tiles are handmade. Reclaimed terra-cotta has generally been made by hand because of its age, but check this too if you want to be sure you are buying a craft rather than a mechanized product.

There is often confusion about the difference between terra-cotta and quarry tiles. In fact the two are made from different clays, but the most significant difference is that they are fired at different temperatures. Quarry tiles are fired to a much higher temperature, which causes them to vitrify to a certain extent. This means that they are less porous than terra-cotta, much harder, less prone to size variations between one tile and the next, and less likely to be warped. They look, and indeed usually are, machine-made, which is not to say that they are not of as good a quality as terra-cotta, simply that handmade and hand-finished tiles look different and more rustic. Quarry tiles appear flatter, less rustic and more regular than terra-cotta. They may also be glazed.

The finish and texture available today on tiles varies from the high gloss of a thick smooth glaze, through the metallic sheen of a luster glaze, to a matte, unglazed surface, which may be rough or smooth. Glazes vary in strength (darker colors tend to be softer), and some glazed tiles are generally less hard-wearing over many years than unglazed ones. Ask your supplier for detailed information in this respect. Unglazed earthenware tiles are matte in their natural state and need to be sealed if they are to be resistant to dirt and grease. Some are sold presealed—a detail that is worth checking with your supplier. If they are not already sealed you can do this yourself without much trouble, or get a professional to do it. Alternatively you can simply leave them to absorb the dirt for a rapid aged, distressed effect (see section three, Practicalities, for basic information about sealing). Some stone and slate

OPPOSITE Light streams down into this courtyard interior. The floor is paved with green and white tiles in a pattern that frames the central fountain and echoes the green of the hanging plants.

LEFT An "antique" effect created on ceramic floor tiles with contemporary glaze technology.

tiles may also need sealing if you want them to retain something like their original, unmarked appearance. They may also have a rough rather than a smooth matte surface.

Tiles are available in a mouthwatering array of colors. Apart from the relatively few types of glazed tile that are suitable for use on floors, the colors you can choose from tend to be the colors of the natural materials from which the tiles are made. There are exceptions to this—encaustic tiles for example, where the color is not applied to the surface but goes right through the tile. If you do decide to limit yourself to unglazed tiles, the range of colors is still tantalizing, from green, blue and grey slate, through the many colors of marble, to the rich variations of reds, pinks and yellows in terra-cotta.

Just as you would when choosing paint for the walls, use the colors of a tiled floor to blend or contrast with other colors in a room, such as curtains, chair and sofa covers, pictures and objects. In a kitchen or dining room, do not overlook the color or colors of the china off which you eat, as this is an important part of the decorative scheme. If the tiled floor is to provide a background for rugs, take their colors and the style and intricacy of their patterns, if any, into account, too. Look out of the windows of a room and consider whether you want the color of your floor to contrast or blend with what you see—be it a brown roofscape, massed buildings in red brick or grey stone, or a lush landscape of green fields.

White is, of course, a useful and popular color in interior decoration, but needs to be used carefully on floors because it shows dirt and marks more dramatically than any other color.

The drama of white means it can be used to stunning effect, and will be less trouble in practical terms in a household without children, animals, or direct access to the outdoors, such as a city apartment with an internal entrance. In a house, especially in the country, it is probably best suited to an upstairs bathroom, a room in which people will usually be wearing soft shoes or slippers.

All these elements in a tile's appearance—material, finish, texture and color—together with others like shape, size and pattern must, of course, be related to the function and style of the room in which the tiles will be laid. This in turn relates not only to the overall decorative effect of the room but also to the style of your whole home, and the period in which it was built. In the country, is your home a rough-and-tumble country cottage, or does it have a sophisticated interior with fine antique furniture? Perhaps it is a combination of the two, with some family rooms and others containing your more precious and fragile furniture and possessions. Does it have low beamed ceilings, or is it a spacious Georgian rectory or townhouse with high airy ceilings and tall windows that flood the rooms with light?

If you live in a small house or apartment, you can help to create a sense of spaciousness by running a tiled floor through several small spaces or rooms. Do not use a border, as this will draw attention to, and appear to shrink, the perimeters of the room. In a family house, tiles are ideal in entrance halls, bathrooms, passages and the kitchen—as indeed they are in any home.

In a town or city, is your home a Victorian terrace house, or a cosy attic flat? Is it a twentieth-century period home—midcentury ranch perhaps—or a high-tech modern space for living? Does it combine living and working areas with different practical and aesthetic requirements? It is always a good idea to take a metaphorical step back from your home and consider it objectively in terms of its form and function. You will probably find that decisions about the type of tile to lay in various rooms and spaces become easy to make, or make themselves with little or no effort on your part, leaving you to enjoy the pleasure of exploring the great choice of tiles available.

RIGHT AND ABOVE Modern terra-cotta tiles (above) laid in slightly staggered rows to allow the use of a charming little insert tile decorated with a fish. Traditional slate tiles (below) are hard-wearing and handsome.

OPPOSITE Handmade terra-cotta tiles, if sealed and polished correctly, will build up a patina over the years that makes them more beautiful than when they were new.

98

FLOORS: FUNCTIONS AND STYLE

FLOORS
DESIGN DIRECTORY

OPPOSITE Terra-cotta tiles can look as much at home in a contemporary interior as in a traditional one.

W HEN YOU WALK INTO A ROOM, the structural element most exposed is usually the floor. Walls have furniture standing against them, with pictures or cupboards above, and are interrupted by doors and windows. One's eye is rarely led directly up to the ceiling unless it is decorated in a special way. The floor, however, spreads out before you. Its visual importance makes it a powerful element: it can make a positive contribution to the success of a room's decoration, or it can make a mess of it. Alternatively, it can retire quietly and discreetly, leaving some other element of the room to make an overriding visual statement.

Pattern is clearly significant in this context, both on the individual tile and over the floor as a whole. Use it carefully to avoid visual confusion, especially if you plan quite an elaborate floor. Conversely, use pattern to give interest to a plain and simple or empty room. In either case, consider whether these are the only tiles in the room: in a kitchen or bathroom, for example, there may well be other tiles, on walls or other surfaces. If there are to be other tiles, plan the tiling as a whole, linking the different areas to each other and possibly limiting pattern to either the floor or the walls.

A few types of floor tile have pattern on each individual tile—encaustic tiles, for example, and inlaid, medieval-style, craftsman-made tiles. Subtle pattern on a floor may also be the result of the natural color variations and

LEFT AND ABOVE Diamond-sawn slate tiles have a rich variety of pattern in their natural veining and mottling.

Fig. 1

Fig. 2

Fig. 3

Fig. 4

Fig. 5

Fig. 6

Fig.7

texture of the material from which the tiles are made. Organized pattern over the whole floor is usually the result of careful planning. For this you should take plenty of time and equip yourself either with suppliers' catalogs and a book such as this one, which clearly illustrate the wide choice of possible patterns, or with plenty of paper, pencils and colored pens, if you want to design your own floor from scratch. Suppliers' samples, which will give you an accurate idea of size, color and finish, will also help you design your floor.

An initial consideration is the size and shape of tiles you wish to use. There are numerous sizes and shapes of tile available. The most frequent and versatile is the plain square in various sizes. Square tiles are usually laid together in a grid, with sides either parallel to the walls of the room or diagonally, at forty-five degrees to them (see Figs. 5 and 7). Squares can also be staggered, rather than being laid in straight rows, and combined with small square inserts in an instep pattern (see Fig. 10). Another alternative is to lay squares in a regular grid but divided from each other by strips of border (see Fig. 11).

A variation on the square tile is the octagon, which either has sides of equal length, or has four long and four short sides. The latter is really a square with the corners trimmed off

Fig. 8

Fig. 9

Fig. 10

Fig. 11

(creating the four short sides) to allow a small square insert of a different color to be placed diagonally between the larger tiles (see Fig. 8). Hexagonal tiles with sides of equal length are laid together in a pattern that resembles a honeycomb (see Fig. 1), or combined with square tiles with sides of equal length to theirs. Diamond-shaped tiles with sides of equal length are like squares pulled out of shape at diagonal corners. They fit together to make whole intricate floors or border strips (see Fig. 2).

Apart from the square, the other most regular shape is the rectangle. This can be laid on its own in a variety of patterns including the classic herringbone (see Fig. 4), at right angles to each other and separated by small squares in a loose basket-weave pattern (see Fig. 3), or in different sizes and combined with squares of different sizes for a more random effect (see Fig. 6). The rectangle has an elegant variation in the six-sided lozenge, in which each end of the rectangle has been extended into a point. These fit together by themselves in a close-fitting basket-weave pattern, or with squares of various sizes in a number of satisfying patterns (see Fig. 9). There are other, more elaborate shapes of tile—most notably in the Islamic style—which are generally made of glazed stoneware suitable for walls rather than floors. These are described in the following chapter.

Various patterns can be made with plain square tiles of the same size but different colors. They may be different colors because they are made from different materials, or from different types of the same material—red and yellow terra-

cotta, for example. Or they may be manufactured in a choice of colors, like encaustic tiles. Two colors can form stripes in straight lines or diagonals, or the classic checkerboard of alternate dark and light tiles across the whole grid (see illustration on page 107). A double-sized grid can be formed by making alternate squares of four tiles of one color, using either smaller tiles or larger tiles on a large expanse of floor. The whole checkerboard can be laid straight along the room or passage, or diagonally to the walls. The latter arrangement will make a narrower hall look wider, while the former arrangement will help give an illusion of length to a shorter hall, by leading the eye onwards.

With three colors of tiles, a kaleidoscope of patterns becomes possible, generally with an effect rather like tartan or plaid. Set lines of each color either straight or diagonally to the walls, or diagonally across a straight grid. Or form a checkerboard from alternate single or double squares (see page 107) of darker-colored tiles separated by squares of lighter tiles. Alternatively, the squares can be formed from two of each darker color, set diagonally. Three or more colors can also be placed apparently at random, though it is worthwhile planning the "random" effect carefully in advance. Do this by drawing it out first, or make a plan using small cut-out squares of different colors, corresponding to the tile colors you are considering (so that you can order roughly the correct number of each color) and then by laying the tiles out dry and loose on the floor to confirm your design before fixing them in place.

OPPOSITE An impressive kitchen in Milan, where sixteenth- and seventeenth-century tiles have been used to create a contemporary abstract design on floor and walls.

If you are a confident and experienced tiler, or if you are employing a professional tiler—or if you are simply brave and adventurous—you could consider using cut-work tiling. This involves cutting some of your tiles into pieces, usually triangles, either half or a quarter of a tile in size, and rearranging them into a satisfying pattern (see page 108). The edges of each cut piece must be clean and smooth, and the pieces must be fitted back together tightly in their new format, to make the same area as a single uncut tile.

Colored grouting can be used to help create pattern, but the choice of colors available is generally limited to a few pale shades. Mixing your own with pigment of stronger color may weaken the chemical mixture and strength of the grout, and you may also find that the color is streaky because it has not been mixed industrially. Black and dark brown and grey grout are also available as an alternative to white and the pale shades, and are obviously well suited to tiles of darker color. Whatever the color, the grout on a tiled floor is likely to weather into a more neutral shade with use.

A border gives a tiled floor definition and a finished look. Many styles of tile have a border designed to coordinate with them, but it is perfectly possible to create your own border using tiles of contrasting colors and materials. Any shape can be used: large and small squares, the latter possibly in more than one row; diamonds; or tiles of more than one shape (see below).

Finally, borders and changes in color or pattern can be used to manipulate space visually. You can use them to divide a kitchen-cum-dining room, for example, where you want to differentiate between cooking and eating areas. In other circumstances you might want to unify space rather than divide it. In a home of small proportions, you can lead the eye beyond the confines of one small room by continuing the same tiles through from one room to the next. In a room of annoyingly irregular shape, perhaps one with nooks and crannies, use a color change or border to create a regular geometric shape, set in from the edge of the room, as a focus in the center and distraction from the irregularities.

RIGHT AND ABOVE Ideas for tile patterns both contemporary (above) and traditional (right).

BATHROOMS AND KITCHENS

Oᴘᴘᴏꜱɪᴛᴇ These modern mosaic tiles come already formed into squares and rectangles, either plain or with a decorative motif.

O ꜰ ᴀʟʟ ᴛʜᴇ ʀᴏᴏᴍꜱ ɪɴ ᴀ ʜᴏᴍᴇ, the kitchen and bathroom are those where hygiene is most important and where water is most in evidence. Tiles are ideal in this situation, which is why the Victorians used them so enthusiastically to clad and decorate their new hospitals, food halls, dairies and, in the home, their bathrooms and kitchens. In today's homes, it is the kitchen and bathroom that lend themselves to decorating with tiles more extensively than living rooms and bedrooms. These tend to be softer places for relaxing and sleeping, whereas the kitchen is the busier part of a home.

The status of the kitchen has, of course, changed out of all recognition since the Victorian heyday of the domestic decorative tile. It is now as much a room for living in as any so-called living room or sitting room. The kitchen is where the family gathers in the morning and the evening to eat, but it is much more than a domestic office for the preparation and eating of food. It is a social center, where members of the household sit and talk or read or play, if they are children, or watch television. Attitudes towards food itself have changed too, so that the kitchen is a sort of cultural center where the culinary ideas and materials of many countries are available, and the interested cook can relax and be creative while assembling meals for himself or herself, family and friends. As much entertaining now takes place in the

Lᴇꜰᴛ ᴀɴᴅ ᴀʙᴏᴠᴇ Details of mosaic tiles showing a fish (left) and shell (right).

III

OPPOSITE The kitchen of this Mexican home looks welcoming due to the vitality of the tiled surfaces. The colors are all blue, white and yellow, so in spite of the variety of patterns, the effect is still harmonious.

kitchen as in the dining room, a room which in any case is increasingly considered a luxury and even unnecessary.

The bathroom too has changed, from being purely utilitarian, and often cold and uncomfortable, to being a real room, interesting and welcoming and a pleasure to spend time in. The effect of these changes is apparent in the amount of time and effort we put into devising decorative schemes for our bathrooms and kitchens. As with floor tiles, decorated and plain tiles are now available from all over the world, combining the necessary hygienic qualities (which have never gone out of fashion) with beauty.

The importance of hygiene in kitchen and bathroom means that you or your decorator need to consider carefully the type of adhesive and, even more important, the grout to be used. The adhesive needs to be water resistant. There are various types of grout available, such as those recommended for use on kitchen walls and in bathrooms and showers (with added fungicide) and others for kitchen work surfaces. The latter type is an inert compound which will not absorb food particles or bacteria—anything that lands on it can be completely washed off. Check that the one you buy has passed tests that allow it to be used in food preparation areas in places like restaurants and bars where the general public could be affected by a drop in hygiene standards.

One element of decoration that many people consider unsuitably unhygienic in a kitchen, and to a lesser extent in a bathroom, is window dressing. Curtains absorb moisture and grease, and can be a fire hazard. You may decide to do without

and instead use a plain blind or shutters to retain privacy at night, or you may not feel the need to cover your windows at all, if you are not overlooked. In any of these cases, consider framing the window with colored or patterned tiles. Make sure that any cut tiles necessary for a perfect fit are at the corners of the window, not in the middle, or position the frame of tiles an inch or two away from each side of the window to avoid completely the need for any cut tiles.

Kitchens and bathrooms are the rooms in which to use picture tiles. Here they will be properly seen and enjoyed—in most cases picture tiles are unsuited to the heavier wear floor tiles suffer. Picture tiles can be used en masse for a richly ornamented effect that the Portuguese would recognize from their great tradition of cladding whole walls and rooms with a riot of pattern and color; or used in panels and strips to accent particular parts or characteristics of a room; or interspersed with plain white or colored tiles between, which allows the picture on each to stand out and be seen more clearly. Ideal images for kitchens include fresh vegetables and fruit, flowers, ornamental birds; and words like the names of herbs, or Italian or French cooking terms or words for foods. Unless you are vegetarian, fish are another suitable subject; but even if you are a keen carnivore, you might consider pastoral pictures of cows and sheep to be inappropriate in this context.

Before deciding on any set of tiles, however, take a step back and look at your kitchen as a whole. What is its style or mood, and what are the dominant colors? Do you have a wood stove with a colored enamel finish, or enamel-coated cast-iron

Opposite Another Mexican kitchen, this one using modern tiles with severe rectilinear decorations to create grandeur and to focus the eye on the stove, the heart of the kitchen.

Left A contemporary Mexican tile made in Puebla based on a traditional design.

pans? What color are your storage jars? What are the colors and style of the pattern on your china? Can the cabinets be painted in order to create a fresh new color scheme and coordinate with the tiles? If this seems too drastic, is it possible to buy replacement china knobs for drawers and cupboards in a color that links the units to the ceramic tiles? An alternative to the latter plan is to paint or stain wooden knobs, and then protect them with several coats of clear varnish.

Besides the floor, other obvious places in which to put tiles in a kitchen are on the wall above the work surface, and face-up on the counter, forming the work surface itself. On the wall above the work surface, tiles provide a practical, wipe-clean background for potentially splashy activities like beating, blending and mixing. Space on the wall is often limited by wall-mounted cupboards, so fewer tiles are needed to make an impact. A border along the top of the tiles here is less likely to be obscured by storage jars or objects such as small electric appliances than one along the bottom. Borders along both top and bottom create a strong outline and horizontal emphasis that would be especially refreshing in a very small kitchen.

If there are no wall cupboards, a splashback of tiles can be continued up the wall to the ceiling, or it can be limited to a height of four or five tiles, or it can end at any point in between. Considerations are the height of the room and the use to which the wall space is to be put. Shelves for objects or books, pan stand or drying racks, pictures: a low splashback beneath any of these will make sufficient visual impact and be

as practical as a taller one.

If you want to use just a few tiles for maximum impact, limit them to places in the kitchen where they will be of most practical use, such as behind the sink or stove. A panel of tiles consisting of a border framing a picture of flowers in a vase, a colorful exotic bird or a figure in peasant costume, for instance, would be ideal here. So would a patchwork of tiles with the same finish but many different colors, or many shades of one or two colors. If you have collected some Victorian or other antique tiles, and if they fit in with the style and colors of your kitchen, this might be a good way of displaying them, where you will see them regularly and gain maximum pleasure from them, at the same time putting them to practical use. As elsewhere, the color to use most carefully is white. Remember that in a kitchen it will show splashes of dirty water or grease more readily than other colors. Some people consider this a real advantage in hygiene terms since you can easily see what needs cleaning.

Other possible places to use small quantities of decorative tiles are across the front of a stove hood, and along the base under your cabinets. In the latter case, your kitchen really needs to be of the farmhouse rather than the galley type and size, as the tiles will only be seen properly from several feet away. Base tiles also need to be quite tough as they will tend to be kicked in this position. The usual arrangement for the base is to tile it with the same tiles as those used on the floor, but you do not have to stick rigidly to this rule, just as you do not have to limit terra-cotta and other tiles used for flooring

RIGHT Blocks of bold color created by using a patchwork of modern Mexican tiles.

OPPOSITE By contrast, this kitchen is as sleek and shiny as acres of stainless steel can make it. Tiles on walls and floor extend this theme, enlivened with a narrow black and white border.

to the floor underfoot. You can use terra-cotta or marble for the walls above your work surfaces, where you can enjoy their subtle, swirling colors. Terra-cotta will have to be thoroughly sealed; thinner, machine-manufactured tiles may be more practical than thicker, heavier, handmade tiles, as the former are smoother and therefore more hygienic, and their lighter weight will cause fewer problems when attaching them to the wall.

Tiles on work surfaces are a cause of some controversy. Most people whose kitchen countertop is constructed of tiles are very happy with them, but some people regret the choice, not on aesthetic grounds but because of hygiene and practicality. They find the overall surface is not regular and smooth enough to work on easily, and the grouting is never completely level with the top of the tiles, which means that liquids and food particles inevitably get trapped. This is why many people who consider having a tiled work surface decide against it, and choose instead a material such as wood, marble, Formica or stainless steel. However, you need not do without tiles completely if you choose one of these surfaces: a ceramic border or lip can be used to finish it off along the front edge. The same is true in a bathroom, where you may prefer to have basins and bath set into a smooth, wipe-dry surface edged with tiles, rather than a surface made of tiles. Hygiene on bathroom surfaces is not perhaps such a vital issue, however, since you do not eat food prepared on them.

The bathroom is the room where your tile ideas can run riot. It is possible to go to the extreme of actually having your bath and basin lined with tiles. The human body is rounded,

however, and a tiled bath has compulsorily flat surfaces, so be prepared for a little discomfort as the price to be paid for such glorious luxury. Both bath and basin will have to be carefully laid to ensure that the water all runs towards the drain. The more usual use of tiles in the bathroom is on the floor and walls, especially walls immediately above bath and basin. A fully tiled bathroom is intensely practical, since this is regularly the steamiest room in the house as well as the wettest. If you have a shower, either in the bathtub or as a separate unit, consider tiling up the whole wall, even if you do not do this elsewhere in the bathroom. A separate shower made into a cubicle, or an alcove around a bathtub built with partition walling, will be more solid if the partition walls are tiled— and of course the tiles provide an extremely efficient protection against damp.

Completely tiled walls are most luxurious, and can be satisfying in visual terms too, since the unity of the walls draws together what can otherwise look like nothing more than a collection of peculiar china shapes (the basin, toilet, bathtub and so on). The next most unifying arrangement is to tile all walls up to a certain point above the china fixtures, finishing this off with a border. And on the floor, a regular tiled shape like a square or rectangle (or circle, though this is much harder to lay), set among the fixtures, will also have a unifying effect. It helps too if your fixtures are all the same color and match in style. Colors and patterns on the tiles obviously need to be compatible with the fixtures. Now that colors like avocado and burgundy are mercifully out of fashion for bathroom

Opposite For economy, tile bathroom walls selectively rather than from floor to ceiling. Here, some tiles have been attached diagonally to create added visual interest.

Left Some designs from earlier ages are still in contemporary production.

fixtures, and the most popular color is white, this is unlikely to be a problem. This leaves you free to set a mood in your bathroom (and kitchen) with the color scheme you choose for your tiles.

Color can be used to emphasize aspects of space and mood. A small pattern in gentle colors will be soothing; a larger pattern in stronger shades, perhaps a checkerboard of two or more colors, will make your bathroom a wakeful and invigorating place to be. Horizontal or vertical emphasis can be given to a bathroom with stripes created by tiles of alternate colors going along or up the walls, or with tiles that have a pattern with strong emphasis in one direction or the other. An area of solid color will contrast with an area of patterned tiles and throw the pattern into relief.

A border can be placed at any height you choose depending on where you want the visual emphasis. At the lowest level, tiles can be used instead of wooden skirting or baseboards adjoining the floor, which is where the Dutch placed them when they began to use tiles on walls in the sixteenth century. This is effective in a large bathroom with expanses of wall with no fixtures against them—less so in a small room where the line is frequently interrupted. Just above bathtub or sink height (the sink is higher so the line will not be interrupted if the border is above it) is another option. The wall tiling can stop here or continue up the wall above the border.

The next obvious punctuation point up the wall is the height of a low ceiling—seven or eight feet. A border here can

help give an illusion of height if you have a low ceiling, and will give the eye a resting point if the ceiling soars away above it. Alternatively, in a low-ceilinged room place the border at one of the levels below head height in order to distract from the lack of a soaring ceiling. A tile border need not go the whole way around a room if only one area—around the bath perhaps—is tiled to the top: the line can be continued by a dado rail, picture rail or a painted or paper border.

Many bathrooms are small, in which case use either warm colors to create a sense of intimacy, or cool colors and plenty of mirrors to give an impression of greater space. In a cool bathroom the lighting, especially electric lighting, must be well placed and plentiful or the effect will be cold and dingy. Whether you use patterned tiles, one or two colors of plain tiles, or a mixture, it is worth considering your basic color combinations. Some fresh, cool combinations are blue and white (always popular, in any room), black and white, grey and white, cream and green, green and blue, or green and black. Warm combinations include rich yellow with white or cream, rust and coral, or pale and dark pinks and reds. When choosing colors, remember to take your towels into account, and the color of the bedroom out of which the bathroom opens, if that is the arrangement of rooms.

In cities especially, many bathrooms are not only small but internal—that is to say, without a window. A tile panel showing birds or flowers or an outdoor scene—a lush landscape perhaps, or a seascape with boats—will act as a focus in the same way that a window does, while leading the imagination out to wider spaces and thus introducing a sense of fresh air and the outdoors. This will diminish any feeling of enclosure caused by the lack of windows. Whether or not your bathroom has a window, consider placing your tile panel (or panels) opposite a mirror or mirrored wall, to multiply its effect.

Other figurative subjects appropriate for individual picture tiles on bathroom walls are watery ones like fish, fishing, shells, the sea, the seaside and boats. Verdant subjects that will make your bathroom feel like a cool shady bower, such as abundant flowers and swags and garlands of flowers and foliage, are appropriate too. For a baroque effect, use more than one pattern in your bathroom—one pattern, denser and more elaborate, on the side of the bath, for example, and a simpler version of the same on the walls above the bath and round the basin. So long as the patterns and their colors relate closely to each other, the effect will be rich and sophisticated.

Modern life can be exciting but stressful. For many people, especially those whose homes teem with children and animals, the bathroom is almost the only place in the house where they can close and lock the door without being antisocial or feeling irresponsible, and relax completely. A mug of tea or coffee at the beginning of the day or a glass of wine in the evening, partnered by a paperback book (no tragedy if it gets wet), transforms the bathroom into a haven of self-indulgence. Under these circumstances, you may feel your bathroom deserves really special treatment. This could be a large and spectacular tiled panel alongside the bath or on another wall where you can look at it from the bath, or a specially commissioned mural. If you intend to live in the house for a long time, the expense of a mural will be justified. The following chapter, Walls and Decorative Details, gives more information about commissioning special work from an art or craft tiler.

RIGHT Glass tiles create a sleek modern look behind this sink. Tiles are ideal for bathrooms where water is most in evidence.

OPPOSITE A surreal floor tile design in a home in Sydney, Australia.

WALLS AND DECORATIVE DETAILS

OPPOSITE Clever use of terra-cotta tiles to line the seat and back of a bench in the outdoor eating area of a house in Andalusia, Spain.

Floors, kitchens and bathrooms are undoubtedly the parts of the inside of a home which lend themselves most obviously to being tiled. But they are by no means the only places where tiles can be used to great visual and practical effect. Other possibilities fall roughly into two categories: walls, and decorative details. In the case of walls, it is not necessary to go as far as the Portuguese, who have a tradition of lining whole rooms with a vivid display of pattern and color, and still do not hesitate to decorate in this manner today. A considerable impact can be achieved with far fewer tiles, though the blanket coverage approach is undoubtedly dramatic, and can be stunning.

Two ways of covering a wall but not the whole room with tiles, are the mural and the dado. Both are ideal in areas that may come into contact with water or be subjected to the enthusiastic attentions of animals or children. The walls of a narrow hall, for example, where in winter or rainy weather wet umbrellas, rain-soaked outdoor clothes, and snowy or muddy boots are deposited, would be protected by a tiled dado.

The dado is the bottom section of the wall, below a line called the dado or chair rail. A chair rail is generally around the height of the back of a dining-chair; a dado rail may be higher. The Victorians often decorated the dado with much tougher materials than other parts of the wall, in

RIGHT Modern tiles with designs based on seventeenth-century Catalan tiles.

123

recognition of the extra wear and tear it suffers. They covered it with thick, varnished, marbled paper or an embossed, patterned material rather like linoleum—or, of course, with glazed tiles. Instead of becoming worn and marked, the tiled hall could regain its freshness with a mere wipe of a clean cloth. A tiled dado need not be confined to a narrow hall. It would be appropriate in any entrance area at the front or back of a house, or in an entryway or bathroom, especially in a house or mansion block built in the Victorian or Edwardian period or style.

A traditional tiled dado consists of several parts: the dado rail is a pronounced ridge; the wall below is covered with a combination of plain colored tiles, decorated tiles and slips—narrow strips of plain color that act as spacers between one element and another; and at the bottom is the ceramic skirting, which again protrudes and protects the last few inches of the wall in the same way as a wooden skirting or baseboard. A less traditional dado of tiles is simply the lower section of wall covered with tiles. Visually it is a good idea to give your dado a definite top and bottom, perhaps with borders of darker or patterned tiles. Alternatively, the tiles on the body of the dado could be set diagonally, creating a trellis effect, with the tiles at top and bottom running parallel with the floor.

For a real ceramic dado complete with rail and skirting, it would have been necessary a few years ago to go to a specialist ceramicist concerned with conservation work, and even then the job might have been an expensive special commission. No such drastic measures are necessary now, as the manufacture of all the tiles for a full dado has been revived by at least one factory, the historic Jackfield tile works at Ironbridge, Staffordshire, in England, which had its heyday in the reign of Queen Victoria. Using Victorian machinery and methods of manufacture, Jackfield has succeeded in recreating a glowing depth of color that makes some modern tiles look insubstantial by comparison.

The most modern tiled decoration, by contrast, is a panel or mural created especially for you. There are many tile artists who will take on special commissions for anything from a panel of four or six tiles to a mural that covers yards and yards of wall. Some also offer a complete house service, advising you on tiles for all the rooms where you had envisaged them, so that your entire home will have a consistent style.

The difficulty is often in finding tile artists whose work you like. Ideally they should be near you geographically so that you can meet them, see other work they have done and communicate closely with them as your design develops. Word of mouth and personal recommendation are two ways of discovering a suitable tile maker. Art and craft organizations near you may also be able to provide some information, and national organizations are usually happy to put you in touch with their members, who may get work as a result. Another approach is to look in the classified advertisements in interiors magazines and art magazines.

Once you have a list of tilers, telephone them all and ask for illustrated literature about what they do, or visit them in person to see for yourself. Certainly visit a short list of

Opposite Another tiled surround, this time in the Oak Room of Wightwick Manor, whose interior uses designs by William Morris and other Arts and Crafts artists.

candidates after your initial research. Do not be afraid to ask questions, including technical ones. Craftsmen tilers mostly enjoy the educative process and find that receptive customers quickly become enthusiastic about the whole tile making business. If possible, be clear about what you do, or do not, want; and be guided by instinct if you feel the tiler is not listening properly but simply promoting his or her own ideas.

If you are lucky enough to have an indoor swimming pool, this would be an ideal place to have a mural. It could either show a figurative scene—anything from a seascape with boats to a lush green landscape—or a fantasy such as the underwater world of Neptune and his followers, or it could be a dynamic abstract design of shapes and colors. Think hard about what you really want; if possible look at other murals, and choose a tile artist whose work is compatible with the style of mural you envisage. If you commission a smaller mural, consider having it mounted on a panel and fixing this to the wall, rather than attaching the tiles directly. In this way you will be able to take it with you, if or when you move house. And do not forget that tile makers will usually be happy to make you tiles for use anywhere in your home, not only in decorative panels.

Fire surrounds and fireplaces are always a focus of attention in a room, and provide the ideal setting for a small collection of tiles. Larger numbers can be used to face the inside of an inglenook fireplace, if you have one. In summer, when there is no fire in the grate, the tiles can provide alternative interest, whatever the size of your fireplace. In winter, people instinctively gather round a crackling fire, for the warmth and

because its noise, light and movement draws them to it. Contemporary speculative house builders are once again installing fireplaces after decades of believing them unnecessary, because they have realized that their customers like the feeling of coziness and welcome an open fire gives to a room.

If you are installing a fireplace in the Victorian style, with a cast-iron surround including mantelpiece and basket, and a panel of tiles inset down each side, consider the colors and patterns already in the room before choosing. Such fireplaces generally have the tiles already installed, but it may be possible to make your own choice of tiles. In either case, you could construct a tiled hearth to tie in with, but not compete with, the colors and pattern of the fireplace tiles. If the latter have a bold blue and white floral pattern, for example, your hearth could consist of tiles which are predominantly white with a small motif in blue in the corners and perhaps in the middle.

Some of the most interesting Victorian fireplaces have panels that contain not rows of patterned tiles but tile picture panels. The five or six tiles on each side together make up a complete picture with subjects like vases of flowers or personifications of Peace and Plenty. If you are constructing a modern fireplace, or filling the surround within a wooden chimney piece, you could follow the same idea. You could commission a tile artist to decorate panels or a complete surround of tiles with a subject relevant to you—even a portrait of your home and family. Alternatively, there are so many decorative tiles already on the market, from bright,

127

hand-painted peasant creations to elegant tiles in the blue and white Dutch style, that there should be no difficulty in creating a fire surround that exactly matches your taste and your room.

An unusual and rare form of Victorian cast-iron fire surround had detachable metal "wings" on each side of the grate, each containing a tile panel. The purpose of this was to enable you to change the tiles according to the season, or indeed mood. You would be extremely lucky to find a genuine Victorian fireplace of this type today, but it might be possible to commission a craftsman blacksmith to create something similar if the idea really appeals to you.

Two practical points should be considered when choosing and installing tiles for a fire surround. Check the heat resistance of the tiles you wish to use with your supplier. And if you are using tiles with a diagonal design, be careful to attach these with the pattern going the same way on them all. It is astonishingly easy to slip in the odd tile going in the wrong direction, especially near an edge or the bottom. This is equally true, of course, for any panel of tiles, be it in a fireplace, above a kitchen work surface, alongside the bath or in any other room.

If a joiner or builder is making your chimney piece to your own requirements or design, you could ask for a mantelpiece of sufficient thickness to take a narrow border of tiles along the front—either a plain-colored border or one whose pattern complements the pattern and color of the tiles in the surround beneath. Another way of using tiles on a chimney-piece is to

range them along the back of the mantelpiece, where they will be nearly at eye level. Whether or not this arrangement will appeal to you depends to some extent on what you intend to stand on your mantelpiece. If you have a collection of china or glass that you plan to display there, tiles are an ideal backdrop. Engraved glass will come to life in front of a frieze of plain, dark-colored tiles, and patterned china can be provided with a backdrop of tiles of sympathetic pattern and color. If, however, your mantelpiece tends to become home to a picturesque clutter of postcards, invitations, shells and stones, family photographs and candlesticks which will completely obscure the frieze of tiles, you might feel they are wasted there.

There are many other places in a home where a small number of tiles can be used to great practical and decorative effect. Bedroom hand basins generally need a splashback to protect the wall behind, for which a small panel of decorative tiles is ideal. A basin in this setting wants either to melt as unobtrusively as possible into the room's decorations or to be made an object of interest. You are sure to find that tiles fulfill either of these requirements.

One simple way to make an interesting splashback is with a panel of plain, glazed tiles, about the same width as the basin, edged all round with a patterned border. The plain tiles in the center could be the same color as the basin china. Depending on how much water you imagine the basin users will splash about—which may be plenty, if they are children—you could also cover the area of floor immediately beneath a pedestal or bracket basin with tiles. This "mat" of

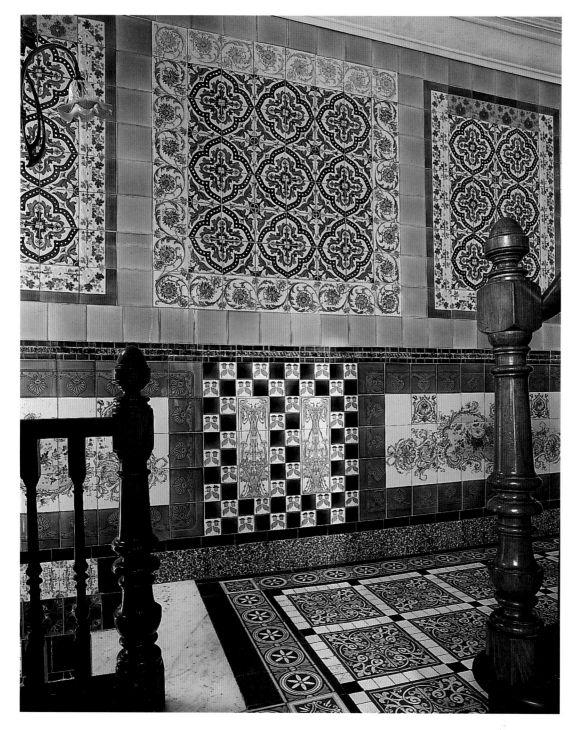

LEFT The Victorian age is well known as a period of inventiveness and enthusiasm and this hallway demonstrates this perfectly. Every available surface has been tiled in a riot of pattern and color, showing the Victorians' love of floral motifs, checkerboard pattterns and borders.

tiles needs to be several inches wider and deeper than the basin, and stretch back to the wall, to be really effective in practical terms.

Indoor window sills decorated with tiles look unusual and attractive, especially if your curtains are unfussy or if you prefer a blind or shutters to window dressing or drapes. Make sure that you start with a whole tile in the middle at the front, or room edge, of the sill, where the eye is instantly drawn. Any pieces of tile should be at the sides and back. In the same way, a whole window embrasure can be lined with tiles, which will help reflect light into the room. As described in the previous chapter, Bathrooms and Kitchens, a whole window can be framed with tiles. This is easiest to do if the window is small, but larger tiles can be used to frame bigger windows and even doors. A doorway with a surround or architrave which is an arch of patterned tiles becomes a dramatic entrance or exit, attracting the eye and leading it on to the room or space that it frames.

Furniture can be built around tiles, or embellished with them, or given a new lease of life. For centuries, furniture has been designed around panels of ceramic decoration. The Victorians, and especially the Arts and Crafts artists, were fond of chairs, sideboards, tables and other furniture which incorporated decorated tiles. Such pieces are still to be found today, or a contemporary craftsman can design and make you your own. Alternatively, raid your attic or cellar, or keep a

look out in junk shops and at auctions for furniture which needs attention and which could be made more beautiful or more useful with the addition of tiles. An old blanket box, for instance, with a cracked and broken lid, can be refurbished with a coat of paint and a tiled top which will transform it into a useful and tough table. A worn tray or small table will be made beautiful again if topped with tiles, though in the case of the tray you need to be satisfied that the tiles are heatproof and not too heavy to make it impractical.

For a really dramatic kitchen or dining-room table, mount a complete panel of patterned or plain tiles on to a board or an old door and provide the top with sturdy legs at the corners, and possibly along the side, depending on the length. Tiles are heavy, especially craft and hand-made ones, and you should be satisfied that they are properly supported. Alternatively, commission a joiner or cabinetmaker to construct a table on which to mount tiles.

Mirrors offer an ideal opportunity for decorating with tiles. Create a frame from border tiles for a smaller mirror, and from whole tiles for a larger mirror, perhaps a full-length one. Finally, single decorated antique and modern tiles can be used and displayed to great effect. Back single ones with felt and use them as stands for hot pots or the teapot at table. Display single tiles on the wall or on a shelf, mounted on a suitable hanging spring or wooden or perspex stand. They will give you pleasure every time you pass by.

OUTDOORS

ONE OF THE JOYS OF HAVING A GARDEN is being able to use it as an extra space for living in when the weather allows. Meals eaten outdoors in the summer sunshine, quietly by oneself or in the company of a crowd of friends and children, have a romantic, Mediterranean aura. Simple food seems special and Sunday lunch a feast. A flat, hard area in the garden is ideal for a table and chairs, which might otherwise sink into the ground and wobble lopsidedly. Another practical consideration not to be dismissed concerns mowing the grass. If your table and chairs are in a grassy area, the person mowing has to move them away and back again, a chore he or she will find a considerable nuisance. This is especially true in high summer, when the grass needs cutting almost every day. The problem is avoided by having a paved area for eating on.

The flat hard area can be near the house, which is practical for carrying things in and out; in a larger garden you could put it in a pretty spot where there are views and shade in case of hot sun. Next to the house, a terrace is an extension of your kitchen or sitting-room—you can slip out to sit and read your newspaper or prepare vegetables at the slightest sign of sunshine and warm weather. If you have small children, such an area is ideal for a sandpit, whose inevitable overflow can easily be swept away.

OPPOSITE Provided they are properly sealed and laid, there is no reason why tiles laid outdoors should not age as beautifully as tiles on floors indoors. They will be subject to different conditions, however, so after a year or two they may look different from the same tiles laid indoors.

133

If your garden is small, perhaps not more than a tiny back yard or a roof terrace in a city, the only sensible way to treat it is to pave it. A postage stamp of grass is not practical (apart from anything else, where do you keep the mower?) and can look silly. Paved areas need minimal maintenance and give a solid surface for terra-cotta pots and other containers in which you can grow anything from vegetables to small trees. Tiles will create a visual contrast with other structural materials in the garden, such as the stone or brick edges of raised beds, and the walls that rise behind them to create the garden's perimeter and give it height.

The materials that usually spring to mind first when planning the bones of a garden are the local stone, flagstones, bricks and gravel. In colder parts of the world, tiles are generally thought of as an exclusively indoor material. Indeed, it is true that they are not suited to great extremes of temperature. But in a temperate climate almost any tile suitable for indoor floors can effectively be laid outdoors, adding hugely to the repertoire of available paving materials. You should be aware, however, that over the years tiles laid in your garden are bound to take on a different look to the same tiles indoors, because they will have experienced different conditions. As long as they are properly laid and maintained they should last equally well.

Apart from the climate, practical details which will affect the suitability of tiles as opposed to other paving materials include their position in the garden, and pollution. Inner-city areas with heavy pollution may not be ideal, especially with porous tiles like terra-cotta, and neither will a position which is overhung with vegetation and tends to be damp. The tiles will almost certainly be affected by algae and become green and slippery. The ideal spot is somewhere dry and sunny.

Terra-cotta, slate and stoneware tiles are those best suited to outdoor use, and should be treated with a top quality waterproof protective sealant on top of the sealing treatment you would give them if you were laying them indoors. The waterproof sealant will be absorbed and block off the pores of the material, forming a skin over it. Once you have done this, surface abrasion is the only maltreatment that may be capable of damaging the tiles—spills should have no serious effect. Every other year, when the warmer, drier weather arrives in spring, give the tiles a thorough scrub with a mild acid and when dry add another coat of waterproof protective sealant. Mild acids include so-called "patio cleaners" which you can buy in garden centers, and any other very mild solution of phosphoric or hydrochloric acid. These will clean dirt, kill algae and cure minor efflorescence.

These materials—terra-cotta, slate and stoneware—do not have to be used exclusively of each other. You can design your terrace in a pattern using any of these together, and also natural stone, to create changes in color and texture. Glazed tiles can also be used outdoors, but their use is more problematical. The most beautiful glazed tiles are often those made by hand, which tend to be deep and chunky, with a thick glaze which gives their color added depth and vibrancy. But of all glazed tiles, these are least suited to outdoor use. If

OPPOSITE This strong geometric pattern of black and white tiles makes an impressive path leading to the front door of a house.

LEFT A witty tiled storefront in Lisbon, Portugal.

moisture penetrates the depth of porous clay beneath the glaze, changes in temperature will cause the tile to expand and contract, which in turn causes cracking on the surface.

Machine-made glazed tiles are more likely to withstand outdoor use than handmade glazed tiles, but they are still not ideal. Thinner, and with a thinner, vitrified glaze, their color is flatter and duller. However, they are less susceptible to moisture penetration and surface damage, and the duller glaze is less likely to be slippery. Handmade glazed tiles can be hazardous if their surface gets wet. It is perhaps better to use glazed tiles sparingly, as a highlight adding color and interest to an outdoor floor, or to create a striking border, rather than as a general paving material.

Areas of paving, paths and paved steps give a garden of any size, but especially larger gardens, visual variety. They bring crispness and an edge, adding definition to the softness and abundance of lawns, flowers and foliage. At the edge of lawns and grassy areas, where these abut flowerbeds, tiles serve a more practical purpose than less regular paving materials. A line of tiles along the edge of the grass makes it easier to mow neatly, and makes it correspondingly less likely that plants trailing over the edge of the bed will be chopped back or otherwise damaged in the mowing process.

In the same way, tiles along the edges of a gravel path help contain the stones as well as adding visual interest and definition to both path and the beds or grass alongside. A path made entirely from tiles can be charmingly patterned between straight tiled edges. Best of all is a network of tiled paths,

between the beds in a rose garden, a potager, herb or kitchen garden, for example. The whole garden can be designed with an overview which allows for the fact that some paths are more important and wider than others, the others being byways off the main axes and vistas. Different tiles can be used for different categories of path, or the same tiles in different sizes, or tiles made in the same material but in different shapes.

A garden on different levels has an inbuilt advantage over a flat one, in terms of visual interest. Steps leading the eye from one level to another are a focus in themselves as well as an introduction to a new view or vista. Narrow steps are mysterious, almost secretive; broad steps which allow two or more people to walk abreast up and down them are generous and welcoming, even romantic. In either case, if there is any sign of the treads of steps faced with tiles becoming slippery and dangerous, scrub and reseal the steps each year rather than every other year.

As with an indoor windowsill or work surface, make sure when laying tiles on steps that the front edge of each step is constructed from whole tiles, with any cut pieces at the back; and that the tiles are laid symmetrically with either a whole tile, or the joint between two whole tiles, in the middle of the step. If an exact number of tiles does not fill the width of the step, fill the edges with pieces of tile of equal width, rather than filling one side only and distorting the symmetry. The same applies to the risers, but here you need not be so conscious of practicality. Because they will not be walked upon, you need not worry about these tiles being slippery, so

137

RIGHT The White Hart
Hotel has a picturesque
tiled panel showing the
synonymous beast
glowing against a dark,
leafy tree.

OPPOSITE Tiles are used
outdoors on balconies,
steps or in courtyards
more as a matter of
course in hot countries,
but are perfectly able to
cope with a temperate
climate.

you can include decorated and colored glazed tiles for consideration when planning the steps' appearance.

Risers are seen in a way that treads are not, and they therefore offer an unrivalled opportunity for decorative detailing. You could decorate the risers with patterned tiles, or pictorial ones, or plain-colored ones, or letter tiles spelling out names and dates, or even a favorite poetic quotation. For neatness and precision, plan the height of each step to accommodate an exact number of the tiles you want to use. The structure of the steps beneath, to which tiles on risers and treads are attached, must be solid and secure, so that no undue pressure is placed on the tiles when people walk up and down the steps. Ideally, the underlying structure should be made from concrete or concrete blocks cemented together. The tiles should then be firmly fixed and grouted in the same way as an outdoor tiled floor. Work from the bottom to the top of the steps, from front to back of each tread and tile each riser before progressing up to begin the next tread.

An outdoor tiled floor, forming a terrace or seating area in your garden should be designed and planned in much the same way as an indoor floor. The same huge range of patterns is available to you, including the classic checkerboard of alternating dark and light tiles, and the variety of terra-cotta shapes such as hexagonals, octagonals and lozenges. But because an outdoor tiled terrace is only used for part of the year and does not have to accommodate a collection of furniture and rugs, you can perhaps allow yourself to indulge in ideas that are a little wilder than you would use indoors.

Borders can be broad and strong, the pattern within can be bolder and more daring. You could draw a maze with tiles of different shades or colors, for instance, or spell out initials or a monogram.

If possible, plan the area as a regular shape—a square or rectangle—and if it is irregular, lop off the odd angles which prevent it from being regular, for the purpose of discovering where the main body or grid of the floor will be. Peg taut strings into the ground along your axes, and be sure that these give you the visual lines you want. When calculating the position of your first tile, allow for the same width of grout joints between tiles as you would indoors.

Tiles outdoors must be laid with meticulous care to ensure that there is no possibility of moisture being trapped underneath. This will shorten the life of the tiles by swelling in icy weather and causing cracking. Tiles should never be laid straight on to soil or sand. Dig the area out to a depth of 15 cm (6 in) and fill it with broken rock or brick, which will ensure efficient drainage underneath the paving. Pack this down thoroughly, lay a generous screed of concrete, and bed the tiles while the concrete is wet. Finally, grout with a product which is suitable for outdoor use.

Besides sealing the tiles thoroughly, you could take the extra precaution of sealing them individually before you lay them. It is also possible to seal the bottoms, to protect against moisture penetration, but this should not be necessary if the tiles are properly laid. The ideal weather in which to create your outdoor tiled area is obviously warm and dry. Rain will

OPPOSITE Tiles provide the ideal flooring for a conservatory. Underfloor heating can be installed to keep a conservatory warm in winter and make it a treat to walk on barefoot.

LEFT The tile making tradition continues in Portugal today; this house front is an example of contemporary taste.

ruin the process. You should also be certain that the tiles themselves are completely dry before beginning. Water is an important consideration, however, and must be taken into account. When it rains, where will the water go? You do not want it to lie or be trapped on the paving. Use a level to slope your tiles very slightly towards a drain or gully or other place such as a well-drained flowerbed where the water will be able to escape or may even be useful.

The conservatory is a popular addition to modern homes: a room which allows you to enjoy the outdoors even when the weather forces you to stay indoors, but which opens out to become part of the garden when the weather is fine. Tiles provide the ideal flooring in a conservatory. The floor should be planned taking into account the style and function of the room out of which it opens, the type of garden it adjoins, and the size and style of the conservatory itself. Otherwise the floor should be planned and laid in the same way as an indoor floor. As with an indoor tiled floor it is important to give special consideration to the focal point where you want to see whole tiles, not pieces.

LEFT A pattern created by imaginative use of antique encaustic tiles, probably dating from around 1870.

SECTION 3:

PRACTICALITIES

THIS CHAPTER IS AN OUTLINE of the basic techniques involved in laying and fixing tiles. It may make tiling seem impossibly difficult and problematic, but in the long run it really is worthwhile doing the job properly. After all, a well-laid tile floor or wall will last a long time. And you will probably find not only that it is not as complicated as you thought, but also that you get better and quicker at it as you go along. Begin your tiling career in a spot which is not the most visible, and by the time you get to the showpiece area in the middle of the floor or the bathroom wall, you will almost be an expert. Alternatively, if you are not confident of undertaking a large tiling project and the prospect of doing it yourself gives you sleepless nights, get a quotation for the work from a professional. The cost of getting a professional to do your tiling may not be great when considered in terms of the many years of use you will get from the tiles, especially if you have to buy or hire equipment to do the job yourself. But beware, not all general decorators are necessarily good at tiling. Ask to see other tiling work they have done and ask your tile supplier if they have a list of recommended tilers in your area.

There are whole books devoted to tiling covering every minute detail, and some decisions you will have to make are a matter of personal taste. The following is intended only as a general guide, not a gospel. Remember to read carefully the manufacturer's instructions on the packages of adhesives, grouts and sealants, and above all, remember the golden rule of tiling which is to keep everything meticulously clean and orderly as work progresses. Many of the practices for fixing wall tiles are the same as for floor tiles, so read both sections even if you are only applying tiles to the walls. You will find that instructions for walls quite often say "As for floors...."

For both floor and wall tiling there are two golden rules. The first is to satisfy yourself that the tiles you have chosen are suitable for the job you intend them to do. A reputable supplier should be happy to discuss this with you in detail, and also the method and materials for applying them. The second rule is not to rush. Take plenty of time to plan and prepare your walls and floors, and then to fix the tiles themselves. Archaeologists dig up tiles that have survived centuries; your tiles will be with you for a long time, and it is well worth taking the time to get them right.

FLOORS

EQUIPMENT

For preparing the subfloor you may need various concreting and woodworking tools, depending on the extent of the work. For planning the layout of tiles on the floor you need a tape measure, string, chalk and a right angle. Fixing requires an adhesive trowel with a ¼-inch notched edge, and a level. You will need cutting tools (the heavier types can be rented) for fitting tiles around the edges of the room, and a selection of cloths, sponges and a paintbrush or roller, all clean and new, for sealing unglazed tiles. For grouting you need a hard implement like a piece of curved or bent narrow-gauge metal piping, to press the grout into the gaps between tiles. And finally you need a polisher or cloths for waxing, and a broom and mop for maintaining your newly tiled floor, as appropriate for the material from which the tiles are made.

THE SUBFLOOR

Whatever it is made of, the floor to be tiled should be level, clean, dry and free of dust, grease and loose material. This applies also to walls to be tiled.

TYPES OF SUBFLOOR

CONCRETE SCREED

When tiling on to a new screed, a period of at least one week for each 1-inch depth of concrete should have elapsed to ensure that the screed is completely dry. Further time may be necessary depending on the weather and site conditions.

WOOD

Suspended floors should be rigid and stable enough to bear the additional load. The floor can be stiffened by fixing ½- or ¾-inch "shuttering" plywood over the existing wood, screwed down at 6-inch intervals. Prime the surface of the plywood with a coat of an aqueous-based copolymer (a general purpose primer and flexible compound which helps the adhesive cope with a certain amount of vibration). Do this before fixing the tiles, or add it to your adhesive. This will increase its durability and flexibility, and is also useful for laying tiles on a work surface in a kitchen.

EXISTING CERAMIC TILES

Ideally, old tiles should be lifted; but if they are completely sound, the new tiles can be laid over them. Existing glazed surfaces should be roughened with a sander to provide a key for the adhesive.

OTHER TYPES OF EXISTING FLOORING

Remove vinyl, cork and linoleum floors. Any bitumen left on the subfloor should be covered with a levelling compound such as a strong cement used in a thick liquid state.

BUMPS AND HOLLOWS

Irregularities on the floor to be tiled can be taken up with a thick-bed adhesive during tiling. If the floor is very uneven, with undulations of more than ½-inch, a leveling compound should be used.

DAMP

Prior to fixing tiles, damp of any kind should be cured and, if necessary, a damp-proof membrane should be installed.

FINISHED FLOOR LEVEL

This will be raised by the thickness of the tiles to be laid, plus an adhesive bed of approximately ¼ inch. Any resulting discrepancy with the levels of adjoining rooms may be resolved by installing wooden threshold strips.

PLANNING

Allow ample time to study the room and plan your work. Tiling usually begins in the corner furthest from the door. If there is more than one door, you will need to decide which is the primary entrance. The following is a method for finding the exact position in which the first tile is to be laid, in a room of regular shape.

STEP 1

Mark the center line of the room from the wall of the primary entrance to the far end. To do this, measure and mark the midpoints of the wall with the door and the opposite wall. Join these two points with tight string and mark with a straight chalk line.

STEP 2

Find the midpoint of the room by measuring halfway along the center line. From this point, lay tiles on the floor along the center line and going away from the door, without fixing them and allowing for the gap where the grouting will go (usually ¼- to ½-inch, depending on the size of the tiles). This will show you where the last whole tile on this axis will come. Using string or chalk, mark a line across the room at a right angle to the center line, along the outer edge of this last tile.

STEP 3

Lay tiles along this new line (loose, allowing gaps for grouting, as before) towards the corner of the room. This will show you the position of the last whole tile on this axis, which is in fact where your very first whole tile should be laid on adhesive.

STEP 4

As a check on the position of this first tile, mark a third line on the floor, along the outer edge of the tile, and make sure that you have a right angle and that this new line is parallel with the room's center line. You can do this by measuring between the two lines at each end of the room and checking that the measurements are identical.

IRREGULARLY SHAPED ROOM

With an irregularly shaped room, proceed as before after making the following adjustment. Create a regular shape with a right angle in each corner, within the room, using measuring tape, string and chalk, by cutting off triangles and any other shapes which distort the rectangle. When you have laid the tiles loosely on the floor (Steps 2 and 3 above), stand in the doorway and move around the room, to check that the tiles create the right visual lines for the room. It is no good being technically correct if the lines of tiles appear visually to be going off at an angle.

LAYING SQUARE TILES DIAGONALLY

When you have found the midpoint of the room (Step 2 above), lay two square tiles diagonally on the center line so that a corner of each is almost on the midpoint, and the center line also goes through the diagonally opposite corner of each. Remember to leave space for grouting between the tiles as before. Mark a line from wall to wall along the edge of the tile furthest from the door, and proceed as above to find the position of the last whole tile, which will be the first to be fixed down. Make the same checks on your right angles and parallel lines as you would if laying the tiles straight.

FIXING

Prior to fixing, check that the tiles are clean, dry and generally of good quality. Shuffle the batch to ensure that any color and tonal variations are well mixed. Do this with wall tiles too, if and when you do your wall tiling. Floor tiles are usually fixed with a thick-bed adhesive using the solid bed method as follows:

STEP 1

Using an adhesive trowel, spread an area of around one square yard to a depth of approximately $\frac{1}{6}$ inch. Handmade floor tiles may be irregular or even bowed and may therefore need a greater depth of adhesive in order to accommodate tiles of different thicknesses and level out potential irregularities in the finished floor surface. Some slate tiles vary considerably in thickness and are best laid on a sand and cement screed mixed in the ratio 3:1. Glazed insets used with terra-cotta floor tiles can be laid $\frac{1}{12}$ to $\frac{1}{10}$ inch below the terra-cotta in order to minimize wear on the glaze.

STEP 2

Butter the back of the first tile to be laid with a further $\frac{1}{12}$ inch of adhesive, and place it in the starting position. When laying thin, machine-made or quarry tiles on to an even surface it may be possible to use a thin bed ($\frac{1}{10}$ inch) of adhesive, without having to butter the back of the tile.

STEP 3

Push the tile home firmly with a slight twisting movement to spread the adhesive and force out any air beneath the tile. Place the next tile adjacent to the first, allowing for the width of the grout joint and repeat this sideways and along, until the square yard is filled. All the tiles should be soundly bedded in the adhesive without any space for air underneath. Be careful not to allow any adhesive on to the surface of the tiles. If any appears, wipe it away immediately with a clean damp cloth. Check the floor with a level and a straight wood batten as you progress.

STEP 4

When the square yard has been tiled, prepare another similar area and tile it, and continue in this way until you have covered the floor with whole tiles. The remaining perimeter area should now be prepared and tiled with cut tiles (see Cutting, below).

CUTTING

It is possible to cut some thin, machine-made floor tiles using no more than a simple scoring and snapping tool. Mark the surface of the tile where it is to be cut, and firmly score down this line with the tungsten carbide wheel. Use the jaws of the cutter to make a clean break.

Most floor tile types are too thick and tough to be cut in this way, requiring more robust and sophisticated tile-cutting equipment. In general, an angle grinder (rented, or bought from a hardware store) will do the job. Simply mark the tile where you wish to cut it and run the cutting disc along the marked surface three or four times until the tile can be snapped. Rough cut edges should be smoothed and finished with a sanding block or, in severe cases, by rubbing the tiled edge with a broken piece or the edge of another tile.

If your tiles are particularly tough or thick, or if you are tiling an exceptionally large area, you could make your task easier and quicker by renting a water-cooled diamond cutter. Alternatively, ask about a tile-cutting service at your supplier or local tile shop.

SEALING UNGLAZED TILES

Most unglazed tiles need to be sealed in order to protect the porous surface, but exact methods and timing depend on the material from which the tiles are made. Whatever the material, it is vital to make sure that your tiles, and the room, are completely clean and dry before you begin the sealing process. If they are not, you may actually seal in dirt, dust and moisture which could impair the floors final appearance. If your tiles are damp, stand them on end in a well-ventilated area to dry thoroughly before laying. This may not be possible, in which case lay them and keep them clean but do not seal them until they are completely dry. Likewise, all equipment must be kept immaculately clean and materials such as brushes and cloths should be new and previously unused. Use a good quality sealant, preferably linseed-oil based.

Sealing usually takes place in two stages. The first seal is applied once the tiles are fixed but before they are grouted. The second seal goes on over the whole floor after grouting, once the grout has hardened and is completely dry. With sufficient space and time, you could alternatively seal your tiles individually before laying them. Another vital point is that the sealant must penetrate the tile. If you use too much and allow the excess to lie on the surface, it will harden and spoil. All sealants take a few days to harden fully once they have penetrated the tile, so keep traffic on your new floor light for at least the first week.

The following is a guide for sealing the various different materials from which floor tiles are made.

TERRA-COTTA

Before you begin sealing the floor, test some sample tiles for porosity, to give you some idea of how much sealant they absorb. Apply the first seal evenly with a clean paintbrush or paint roller (do not pour it on directly). Especially porous types of terra-cotta may need two or three coats of sealer at both first and second seal. Work the sealant into the surface so that the tile appears matt again within between two and ten minutes. If the tile is matt in under one minute, use the sealant a little more liberally. Within twenty minutes of applying the sealant, check that there is absolutely no surplus remaining on the surface of the tiles. This is extremely important. Wipe away any surplus with a clean dry cloth.

Once the grouting has dried completely, give the floor a second seal by repeating the sealing process. Take great care not to apply too much sealant as the tiles will now be less porous. As before, make sure that you remove any surplus sealant from the surface.

RECLAIMED TERRA-COTTA

It is quite likely that these tiles will recently have been cleaned by the supplier so take extra care to make sure that they are thoroughly dry before you start sealing. They may also be extremely dense due to years of wear. Test some samples for porosity and if they do not readily accept the sealer, mix it 1:1 with white spirit. Otherwise, seal in the same way as new terra-cotta.

QUARRY TILES

It is not strictly necessary to seal these tiles but sealing will give the floor added protection and make maintenance easier. Mix a good quality linseed oil sealant with white spirit in the ratio 1:1 and give the tiles a single coat, worked well into their surface.

ENCAUSTIC TILES

A few years ago these required a complicated sealing process with several steps in order to make them waterproof. No longer—the new generation of encaustic tiles needs only one coat (or two if the floor area takes hard wear). Make sure you use a suitable type of sealant. Ideally this should be a water-based acrylic sealer of the type which undertakes to provide an anti-skid, self sheen, stain finish. The best sorts do not need buffing afterwards. Read the manufacturer's instructions. Probably they will tell you to pour the sealer on to the floor and spread it in one direction with a clean cloth. If you are applying a second coat, allow the first to dry for about 20 minutes. The sealer will probably need a few days to cure or harden before it is water resistant.

MARBLE

Marbles vary hugely in finish—some are already highly polished. Consult your supplier about treatment appropriate to his or her tiles. Rough marble can be sealed with two coats of an appropriate sealant once the grouting is hard and dry and the floor has been washed clean and allowed to dry. The second coat should be added before the first is fully dry.

SLATE

Like marble, slate can be sealed in one continuous process. Pour an acrylic polymer that will give a protective surface coating on to the tiles and spread in one direction only with a lint-free cloth or paint roller. Do not rub or buff. Allow it to dry for about twenty minutes then apply a second coat at right angles to the first, to ensure an even coverage.

LIMESTONE

Special limestone sealant is available, as unsealed limestone is susceptible to staining. Read the manufacturer's instructions carefully. The first coat goes on before grouting, applied thinly and worked into the tiles with a new paint brush. After about an hour it should have dried sufficiently to allow light traffic and grouting. When the grout is completely dry add a second coat covering the grouting as well, and leave to cure for about forty-eight hours.

GROUTING

This is the process of filling the spaces between individual tiles and thus completing the floor surface. The purpose of grouting is to strengthen the overall floor, and in order to do this the grout must support the edges of all the tiles fully. This means filling the gaps completely, level or almost level with the top of the tile, not sunk down leaving vulnerable edges exposed.

Depending on site conditions, the fixed tiles should be left for between twelve and twenty-four hours, to allow the adhesive bedding to dry out. The joints should be clean, dry and free of loose debris. Check the manufacturer's recommendations to ensure that your grout is suitable for the type of tiles and situation. For example, sandstone grout is useful for most domestic tiling and with more rustic, textured floor tiles. Grey grout is good for glazed tiles where you will want a more precise grout joint but you should use it with care with unglazed tiles as the fine particle composition carries a higher risk of staining the tiles. Sand and cement mixed 3:2 can make an effective grout; use fine washed sand for a sandstone appearance or a sharp sand for a more rustic look. Joints of more than ½ inch will need a wide-joint grouting compound.

In general it is better to fill the joints by a pointing process, pressing it neatly into the gaps, rather than a spreading or slurry technique. Porous, unglazed tiles which could be stained by excess grout should certainly be grouted by pointing, and their surface must be kept clean at all times by being wiped with a damp, clean sponge. Push the grout well down into the joints to prevent air pockets and help the grout set hard. Then smooth off the joints with a hard implement slightly narrower than the grout—a small piece of narrow, bent metal pipe (not copper) would be suitable.

As soon as the floor is finished and the grout has completely dried, the tiles should be thoroughly brushed to remove any stains or fine dust particles. If necessary, wipe them with a damp sponge and leave them to dry.

MAINTENANCE

All floors benefit from some maintenance, if only sweeping and wiping over with a mop and light detergent once in a while. Unglazed tiles, particularly terra-cotta which improves with wear, need a little more maintenance.

Polish terra-cotta with a good quality wax polish in paste form, use it sparingly and finish it with plenty of effort to build up a hard protective finish. A first polish should be given to the finished floor just a few hours after the final seal, and two more in quick succession; then once a week for the following four or six weeks to build up a hard-wearing surface.

Some types of presealed terra-cotta require a maintenance kit which should be available from the supplier and used as instructed. Quarry tiles can be polished with a good quality wax. Encaustic, marble and slate tiles should be maintained with a low-alkaline detergent diluted with warm water. Rinse the mop regularly in the solution to remove dirt as it accumulates. For a shine on slate tiles, finish with wax polish.

WALLS

EQUIPMENT

You will need the same equipment as for floor tiling, with the exception of sealing equipment (assuming you are using glazed tiles). In addition you will want wood battens measuring about 2 by 1 inches and a plumb line, for planning the layout of your tiles, a $\frac{1}{10}$-inch tiling trowel and adhesive spreader for fixing, tile pincers or a hacksaw fitted with a multi-directional tungsten carbide blade for cutting curves and other complex shapes, and a rubber squeegee or float (not metal which could damage the glaze) for grouting.

WALL PREPARATION

Tiles can be fixed to most walls. As with floors, the surface must be properly prepared and be even, sound, clean, dry and free of dust, grease or any loose material.

Unrendered and rendered walls

Concrete block and other types of unrendered wall should be tiled using a thick-bed adhesive to allow for the uneven surface of the wall. Tiles can be fixed directly on to sand and cement render (4:1 using Portland cement), which in fact is an ideal base. Newly built or rendered walls will need at least fourteen days to dry out thoroughly before tiling can begin.

Plastered, papered and painted walls

Loose plaster must be made good, and new plaster should have been completed at least four weeks before tiling and be primed with a plaster primer. Old wallpaper should be stripped. Sand gloss paint to provide a key for the adhesive, and remove any peeling gloss or emulsion paint.

Wood

Seal walls of wood or wood composite construction with a bonding agent, and allow it to dry before tiling.

Existing tiled walls

Old tiles do not have to be removed, so long as they are secure and the wall underneath is sound. If necessary, sand to provide a key for adhesive.

Bumps, hollows and damp

Serious defects in the wall surface should be smoothed and made good. The wall must be completely dry—any underlying damp problem must be solved before fixing tiles to it.

PLANNING

Take plenty of time to do this. The most important part of planning wall tiling is to decide where the focal point is on the wall or in the room and to ensure that your view won't be obscured by objects placed in front of the tiles. This is the place where you want an immaculate row of whole tiles, not a strip of tile pieces that have had to be cut to fit leftover space. On a kitchen wall this will be either immediately above the work surface, or possibly just below the wall cupboards, where clutter on the work surface will not hide the tiles. In a bathroom, the place where you feel it is most important to have whole tiles rather than pieces may be just below the ceiling, or above the skirting, or, most likely, along the edge of the bath. The choice is entirely up to you and your personal taste. You will have to live with it, so it is worth taking the time to get it right.

Once you have decided on the focal point, proceed in much the same way as for floor tiling, using batons, measure and plumb line to work out where your first tile should be fixed. Use a level regularly to check that the tiles are straight, and remember to leave room for the grouting, when both planning and fixing. Nail battens at right angles to each other creating a corner where the first tile in the bottom whole row of tiles will rest, and don't remove the battens until the adhesive is completely dry. This is to stop it slipping while drying.

FIXING

Use non-slip, water-resistant ceramic wall tile adhesive suitable for intermittently wet areas such as work surfaces, splashbacks, bathrooms and showers. An exception to this is a situation where the tiles may be completely or continuously immersed in water (the lining of a bath, for example). In this case, use a specialist adhesive of a type which is also suitable for fixing tiles on exterior walls and floors.

With an adhesive spreader, apply a thin ($\frac{1}{10}$-inch) layer of adhesive to an area on the wall of about one square yard. With the notched side of the spreader, comb the area to create a ribbed surface of adhesive which will accept the tiles. Position the first tile carefully in the corner formed by the wooden battens and push the tile home firmly with a slight twisting movement to spread the adhesive and ensure that there are no pockets of air trapped behind. Fill the first square yard, then prepare another, and so on, as with floors.

Some machine-made tiles have built-in lugs to pre-determine the space between tiles. With the majority of glazed tiles, however, you will have to use spacers or small pieces of cardboard the thickness of the gap you wish to leave for the grouting. Place these between the tiles as you bed them on to the adhesive. Once you have completed the wall using whole tiles, remove the wooden battens and tile around the perimeter with cut tiles.

CUTTING

As with floors, the tougher the tile, the more sophisticated the tile-cutting equipment needs to be. Machine-made wall tiles can usually be cut easily with a hand-held cutter. Curves and other more complex shapes can be cut out with a pair of tile pincers or a hacksaw fitted with a multi-directional tungsten carbide blade. Rustic and handmade tiles are denser and need to be cut with an angle-grinder, as do stoneware tiles. Mitres or angles across the edges or faces of tiles need a precise corner finish, best provided by a diamond cutter.

GROUTING

Grouting walls is much the same as for floors, except that a spreading technique is better than a pointing one for filling the joints. Use a water-resistant grout and check manufacturer's instructions to ensure that your grout is suitable. In places like showers, use an epoxy grout and in any damp place finish the grout flush with the glazed surface to avoid water seeping behind the tiles. Apply the grout with a rubber squeegee or grouting trowel, working it backwards and forwards across the tiles until all the joints are completely filled. As the grout is drying, wipe any excess smears from the glazed surface with a clean sponge. The space or join between tiles and a bath, basin, sink or worktop should be sealed with a silicone sealant to prevent moisture penetrating behind the tiles.

RESOURCES

National Tile Manufacturers

Dal Tile
7834 Hawn Freeway
Dallas, TX 75217
Tel: 800-933-TILE

Florida Tile Industries, Inc.
2210 A–Z Parkway
Lakeland, FL 33801
Tel: 800-FLA-TILE

Laufen International
6531 North Laufen Drive
Tulsa, OK 74117
Tel: 800-331-3651

Summitville Tiles, Inc.
644 State Route
Summitville, OH 43962
Tel: 330-223-1511

Regional Wholesale and Retail Showrooms

Ann Sacks Tile & Stone
2 Henry Adams Street, Suite 125
San Francisco, CA 94103
Tel: 415-252-5889

APG/Arizona Tile
3535 E. Thomas Road
Phoenix, AZ 85018
Tel: 602-266-4422

Bedrosians (Headquarters)
4285 N. Golden State Boulevard
Fresno, CA 93722-6316
Tel: 209-275-5000
Distributor of imported and
domestic ceramic tile, natural stone
tiles and slabs, Mexican Saltillo,
concrete tile, setting materials, and
glass block. Call for showroom
locations.

Ceramic Tile Design
189 13th Street
San Francisco, CA 94103
Tel: 415-575-3785
Tel: 415-454-0698
   (San Rafael, CA)

Country Floors
8735 Melrose Avenue
Los Angeles, CA 90069
Tel: 310-657-0510

Design Tile & Marble
4112 Stone Way
Seattle, WA 98103
Tel: 206-634-3455

Fred Wiley Company, Inc.
Design Center Seattle
5701 6th Avenue South, Suite 127
Seattle, WA 98108
Tel: 206-767-6502

Globe Marble and Tile Co.
7348 Bellaire Ave.
North Hollywood, CA 91605
Tel: 818-982-4040
Importer of marble, granite,
travertine, and limestone for
commercial and residential projects.
Over three million square feet of
slabs and tiles in stock.

Mission Tile West
853 Mission Street
So. Pasadena, CA 91030
Tel: 626-799-4595

Oregon Tile and Marble
1845 Southeast 3rd Street
Portland, OR 97214
Tel: 503-231-0058

RESOURCES

Antique, Artisan, and Specialty Tile Sources

Alora's Handpainted Tile Murals
5042 Shoredge Drive
Coos Bay, OR 97420
Tel: 541-888-8816
Custom backsplashes and wildlife
murals.

California Art Tile
8687 Melrose Avenue, Suite B
Los Angeles, CA 90069
Tel: 310-659-2614
Exclusive distributors for over forty
custom, handmade, small production
studio tile makers including Blue
Slide Art Tile, Renaissance
Studio/Vida Tile, and Wizard Tile.

The Decorative Tile Works
Jackfield Tile Musuem, Ironbridge
Telford, Shropshire TF8 7AW
Tel: 019-5-288-4124
Reproductions using Victorian
machinery and manufacturing
methods.

Deer Creek Pottery
305 Richardson Street
Grass Valley, CA 95945
Tel: 916-272-3373
Tile pressed from the same patterns
as Julia Morgan used at Hearst
Castle and other locations
worldwide.

Designs in Tile
P.O. Box 358
Mount Shasta, CA 96067
Tel: 530-926-2629
An art tile studio specializing in
custom, historic-style tile, both
reproductions and adaptations
inspired by many historic styles and
designs.

Fire Child Pottery & Tile
1715 CR 12
Rollinsville, CO 80474
Tel: 303-258-7783
Unique, handmade tile inspired by
nature.

McIntyre Tile Company
55 West Grant Street
Healdsburg, CA 95448
Tel: 707-433-8866
Handcrafted and handpainted
    stoneware and porcelain tiles.

Mortarless Building Supply
Company
2707 Fletcher Drive
Los Angeles, CA 90039
Tel: 213-663-3291
Large inventory of antique tile and
reproduction Mexican/Spanish tile
circa 1890-1930.

Native Tile & Ceramics
2317 Border Avenue
Torrance, CA 90501
Tel: 310-533-8684
Reproductions of original Malibu
and Catalina tiles.

Solar Antique Tiles
306 East 61st Street
New York, NY 10021
Tel: 212-755-2403
Original sixteenth- to nineteenth-
century tiles and tile murals,
reproductions of Spanish, Chinese,
French, Islamic, Italian, Dutch, and
Portuguese tiles.

Stonelight Tile Showroom
609 South First Street
San Jose, CA 95113
Tel: 408-292-7424
Handmade tiles from the 1920s and
1930s; porcelains from Italy and
Spain. By appointment only.

The Tile Gallery
200 Main Street
Northampton, MA 01060
Tel: 413-585-0446
Handmade French tiles.

Tile Associations and Information

Association of Ceramic Tile
   Manufacturers of Spain (ASCER)
Camino Caminas s/n
12.003 Castellon, Spain
Tel: 34-6-472-7200
ASCER comprises 184
manufacturers from a total of over
225 factories and workshops
involved in ceramic tile production
and decoration activities.

Ceramic Tile Distributors
Association (CTDA)
800 Roosevelt Road, Building C,
   Suite 20
Glen Ellyn, IL 60137
Tel: 800-938-2832
National trade association
representing over 600 distributors
and manufacturers of ceramic tile.

Ceramic Tile Institute of America,
Inc. (CTIOA)
12061 West Jefferson Boulevard
Culver City, CA 90230
Tel: 310-574-7800

Italian Trade Commission, Tile
Department
499 Park Avenue
New York, NY 10022
Tel: 212-980-1500
Provides information on Italian tile
manufacturers.

National Tile Contractors
Association (NTCA)
P.O. Box 13629
Jackson, MS 39236
Tel: 601-939-2071
NCTA provides the names of
member contractors within your area
and publishes references pertaining
to ceramic tile installation.

Tile Council of America (TCA)
P.O. Box 1787
Clemson, SC 29633-1787
Tel: 864-646-8453
Trade association representing
manufacturers; provides ongoing
support information on the proper
installation of ceramic tile.

Web Sites

www.ceramic-tile.com
Information about the ceramic tile
industry with worldwide directory.

www.infotile.com
Forums, directories, catalogs, services.

www.tilenet.com
On-line guide with sections on selecting
ceramic tile, design possibilities,
installation, grouting, and maintenance.

INDEX

AUTHOR'S ACKNOWLEDGMENTS

I would like to thank everyone at Fired Earth for their enthusiasm for this book and for their generous supply of information, but especially Nicholas Kneale, Philippa Humphrey, Alan Berks, Robin Tate and Robin Buchanan. I would also like to thank the following people and organizations for their generous help: Bal (Building Adhesives) Ltd; Juliet Beaumont; Maggie Angus Berkowitz; Felicity Bryan; Georgina Cardew; Professor John Carswell; Sotheby's; Kenneth Clark; John de Falbe; Paul Henry; Tony Herbert; Tiles and Architectural Ceramics Society; Mrs. David Jackson; Sebastian John; Bobby Jones; Rachel King; Hans van Lemmen, Leeds Metropolitan University; Barbara and John Milligan; Sarah Riddick; John Rumsby; Tolson Memorial Museum, Huddersfield; Mrs. Max Selka; William Selka; Simon Sheard; Helen Sudell; Susan Taylor; Odette Wells; Westminster Abbey Press Office; Bronwyn Williams-Ellis; Fenella Willis; Whichford Pottery; Shona Wood.

PICTURE ACKNOWLEDGMENTS

All Fired Earth except:
Arcaid/Richard Bryant 11, 114, 117; Arcaid/Ross Honeysett/Belle 121, Arcaid/Martin Jones 40; Arcaid/Lucinda Lambton 130; Arcaid/Trevor Mein/Belle 120 bottom; Arcaid/Sally-Ann Norman 125; Arcaid/Alberto Piovano 34, 108; Laurie Black 107; Bridgeman Art Library 12, 14, 15, 16, 39, 55 bottom, 62, 70, 72, 76, 77; Christie's Images/© succession Picasso/DACS 1999 80; Dean and Chapter of Westminster Abbey 31; Richard Dennis Publications 61; Edifice 23, 36, 38, 41, 42, 44, 45, 60, 64, 65 bottom, 66, 73, 78, 79, 81 bottom, 82, 134, 137, 138, 141; Robert Harding Picture Library/Rob Cousins 81 top; Robert Harding Picture Library/Ross Ehlert 37 top; Robert Harding Picture Library/Michael Jenner 18 right; Robert Harding Picture Library/John Miller 74, 91, 122; Robert Harding Picture Library/Lizzie Orme 118; Robert Harding Picture Library/E Simanor 17; Robert Harding Picture Library/Adam Woolfitt 19 right, 22; English Heritage 24, 25, 27 bottom, 28, 29, 30 33, 58, 63; Interior Archive/Fritz von der Schulenberg 103; Hans van Lemmen 83; National Trust Photographic Library/Andreas von Einsiedal 56, 68, 126; National Trust Photographic Library/Keith Hewitt 57; National Trust Photographic Library/James Mortimer 67; National Trust Photographic Library/Derrick Whitby 71; Venice Picture Library/Sarah Quill 32; Bronwyn Williams Ellis 84; Elizabeth Whiting & Associates 6, 21, 26 center, 43, 46, 48, 49, 50, 52, 53, 54 left, 88, 92, 96, 113, 129; Peter Woloszynski 139